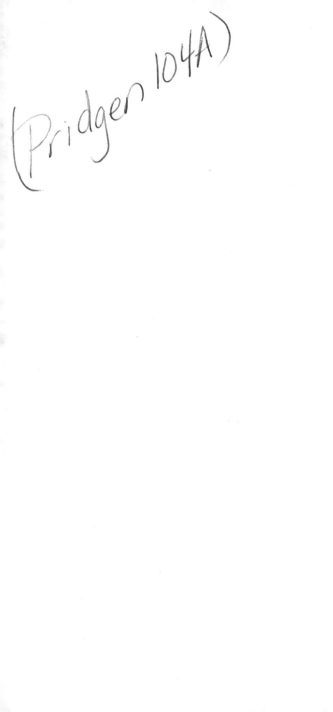

(Pridgen 104A)

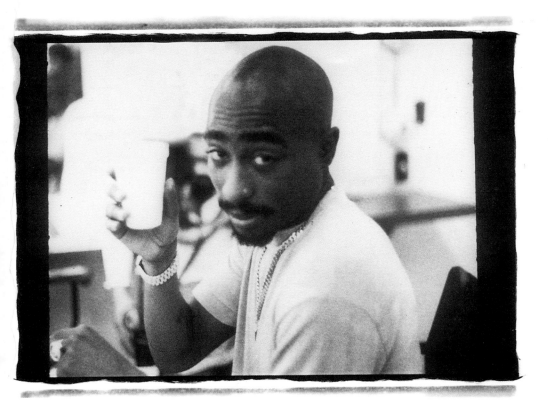

thru
my **eyes**

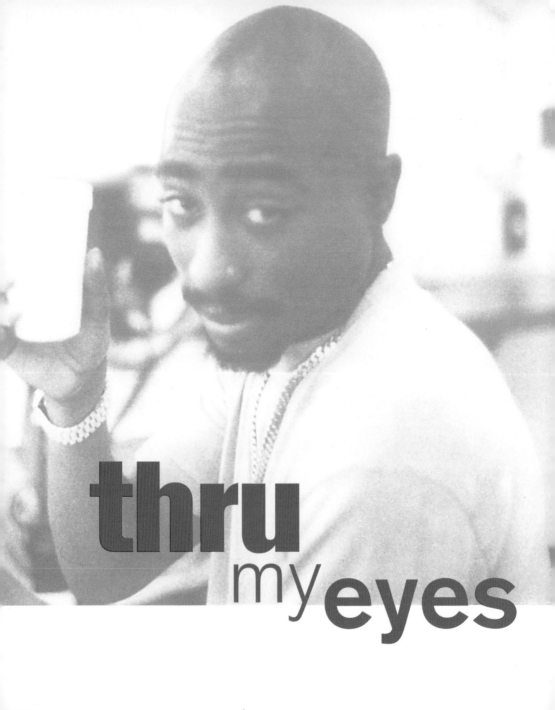

thru **my**eyes

THOUGHTS ON
tupac amaru shakur
IN PICTURES
AND WORDS

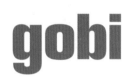

FOREWORD BY AFENI SHAKUR

ATRIA BOOKS

New York London Toronto Sydney

ATRIA BOOKS

1230 Avenue of the Americas
New York, NY 10020

ISBN: 0-7434-5700-5

First Atria Books hardcover printing October 2005

10   9   8   7   6   5   4   3   2   1

ATRIA BOOKS is a trademark of Simon & Schuster, Inc.

Manufactured in the United States of America

Designed by Jaime Putorti

For information regarding special discounts for bulk purchases,
please contact Simon & Schuster Special Sales at 1-800-456-6798
or business@simonandschuster.com.

Dedicated to Tupac's fans.
May his light shine down on all of you.

acknowledgments

I place at the top of my list of acknowledgments the source of all things, the infinite wisdom, God; I thank you for the blessing of life. I thank my father, Jafar; my mother, Manijeh; and my sister, Marjan; thank you for your loving support. Tupac Amaru Shakur, thank you for always speaking your truth as you did, in your work as well as your life. You lived and died like a warrior; your sacrifice has touched us all, and because of it we are better people. Your legacy is a blessing for every future generation. Afeni, thank you for your strength, courage, and wisdom. Thank you for bringing Tupac into this world; you are the creator of the warrior. Every time I see you, my blessings are affirmed; I am here for you. Yaasmyn, I am sorry for your loss. I look forward to assisting you as you tell your story and the story of all who have struggled for a cause. Tracy, I would never have met Tupac if it weren't for you; thank you for the experiences and the lessons, and may you have all the happiness you deserve.

Molly, it feels good to be on the same side as you once again. Kebe, I'm blessed to finally have you as my mate; may we fulfill all our greatest dreams and goals together and thank you for coming back into my life again. Jonny Joon, thank you for all your help and input. Kia Kamran, thank you for all your legal counsel. To my friends and family, thank you for putting up with me and thank you for your loving support. Finally, many thanks to the prophets and teachers of the Way. May we learn from your sacrifices so that we may be guided toward compassion, wisdom, and love.

Over the last nine years, one of the many things that I have come to learn about my son Tupac is that he touched a great number of people. Each and every one of these people had a very unique relationship with him, whether it was through his music, poetry, acting, political beliefs, personal obstacles he had to overcome, or a personal relationship he actually had with them. With each relationship came a story, unique to what he shared with them. Each of these people has a right to tell their story.

I believe that we can learn from one another. Sharing our experiences can create an opening for new possibilities, new understandings, and enlightening us . . . and this is something we all need!

The photos and text in *Thru My Eyes* are a perfect example of this. Gobi had his own special experience with my son and, in sharing his perception, offers a personal view of Tupac that warrants exposure. This book is Gobi's way of honoring my son and sharing his experience with Tupac.

Gobi was one of the few individuals my son chose to work with in his last year of life. Tupac and Gobi worked on a number of projects together and it was during this time that the photographs you find in this book were taken.

I thank you, Gobi, for being my son's friend in life and I appreciate the honor you bring to this project with your integrity in his death.

Peace, love, and respect,
Afeni Shakur

The photos of Tupac in this collection chronicle his last days, from late 1995 to his death, in September 1996. I became a trusted business partner and friend of Tupac Amaru Shakur during the last eight months of his life. He, Tracy Robinson, and I had started a film company called 24/7. I suggested the name because working with Tupac was a 24/7 proposition. Tupac's intention was to create a minority-owned production company and shape it into a force to be reckoned with in the film industry. One week prior to Tupac's death, 24/7 had a potential three-picture deal. I had the pleasure of producing and directing many of Tupac's music videos. I witnessed a young, successful African American man live and die before he received a chance to realize his full potential.

Tupac Amaru Shakur was born June 16, 1971, in New York City. His mother, Afeni Shakur, was arrested along with other members of the Black Panther organization on 189 felony charges that included thirty counts of conspiracy. Although she was eventually acquitted of the charges, Afeni spent eleven months in jail before being released. While out on bail, she became pregnant with her son. I remember hearing stories of how Afeni would fight to get one egg and some milk in order to nourish her son. She once said, "This is my black prince. He's going to save the black nation." Afeni was acquitted thirty-one days before her black prince was born. She named her son Tupac Amaru, after an Incan king; the name means "shining serpent." Tupac received his last name from Mr. Lumumba Shakur, the son of Aba Shakur, two strong and very well-respected members in the Black Nationalist movement. *Shakur* means "thankful to God" in Arabic. One of the most influential male role models in Tupac's adolescent years was Mutulu Shakur, L.A. Dr. Shakur's influence helped to shape Tupac into a man determined to address sociopolitical issues. Dr. Shakur is still incarcerated as a result of aiding Assata Shakur escape the country and for participation in armored-truck robberies.

The majority of Tupac's songs include social and political commentary; even his party songs contain commentary. To simply call Tupac "a rapper" is to misclassify him. He was way bigger than a rapper. He was a great poet, genius artist, social commentator, and the leader of a revolution that evolved from the Black Panther Party. He was the main product of that revolution. When you think about it, he was the greatest product of that movement— he was its main sequela. In a strange way, one could say that the entire movement's main purpose was to create Tupac. It's like all the energy, soul, and power of the Black Panther movement was in his veins.

In the early 1990s, I married an Iranian–American filmmaker. My wife and I produced a spec music video, and in that process I found a passion for filmmaking. A month later, I decided to quit my job as a real-estate agent in Orange County and become a music-video producer. The marriage didn't last, but my newfound passion did. A year after my marriage ended I met Tracy Danielle, who had a small production company, and we started producing hip-hop music videos. Prior to our meeting, she had worked as a production assistant on a Tupac Shakur music video and became so enamored with him that she pledged her undying loyalty to him. Approximately a year after Tracy met Tupac, he was thrown into Clinton Correctional Facility, in upstate New York, on trumped-up rape charges. Suge Knight, the CEO of Death Row Records, paid more than a million dollars (an advance against future royalties) in bail money for Tupac's release. In exchange, Death Row would receive three albums from Tupac. Immediately after his discharge from prison, Tupac went straight into the studio to record *All Eyez on Me* and was put on a rigorous music-video production schedule. On completion of his first video with Dr. Dre, "California Love," Tupac sent his then-assistant Molly Monjauze to find Tracy. He wanted Tracy to produce his next music video, and by default, I was a part of that package. I didn't know much about Tupac prior to meeting him, but, like Tracy, I too was immediately mystified by his persona.

Growing up in Iran, I had often heard of dervishes, people who possess a dynamic, heightened sense of awareness. Much like the shaman or the prophet, these beings are not always accepted by their society or tribe yet often act as powerful forces in shaping it. Tupac possessed such qualities. His artistic contributions to music, film, and poetry are unparalleled. Tupac was an important person not only to African American culture but also to world culture. His music and acting set precedents that have been duplicated by many who have followed in his footsteps. From the moment I met him to the day he died, I considered myself one of his soldiers, and I always will. Tupac was an artist, a warrior, and a poet. During his short life, he achieved those titles with his talent, his persistence, and his tenacity.

Tupac loved to listen to Don McClean, Marvin Gaye, Hall and Oates, Stevie Wonder, David Bowie, Elton John, and Alanis Morissette. He read Shakespeare, Sun-tzu, Maya

Angelou, Kahlil Gibran, and Thomas Moore, to name a few. He was also well versed in world religion.

After Tupac's passing, I read much of his fan mail. Letters poured in from Bulgaria, Russia, Poland, South Africa, and my homeland, Iran. I was amazed by his international influence. Tupac at the age of twenty-five had starred in five feature films and sold millions of albums.

I was privy to a changing Tupac, a Tupac on his way to autonomy and maturity. If he had lived just a bit longer, he would have been able to complete his obligations and move on with his plans; he had just started his own film-production company and record label. He lived the life of a mythological character, like Luke Skywalker surrounded by a fair share of Darth Vaders. Sometimes I feel that he communicates with me in strange ways. His aspirations were never-ending; his spirit, eternal. Meeting him has been one of my life's great pleasures; his death, one of my life's greatest disappointments. I will miss him dearly and I will mourn his death for the rest of my days. He changed me, and because of him I am a better person. May peace be upon him.

In judging Tupac, most people take for granted that he was only twenty-five years old when he died and that he literally grew up under the intense scrutiny of the public eye. During his short life and the time since his death, the media has focused solely on aspects of his character that feed into black stereotypes. What has been neglected, however, is that Tupac was a very sensitive young man deeply affected by the suffering of oppressed people and he had a lot of plans for the future that involved politics, social change, and charity. As time goes on, my respect, admiration, and awe continue to grow rather than die away. I am lucky to have witnessed Tupac's existence, and everyone I know who knew him feels the same. Tupac changed people's lives in a supernatural way.

The first time I met Tupac was on a sunny California day in Malibu. I went to Tupac's beach house with his assistant, Molly. When I arrived, Tupac was having a business meeting while the Outlawz ran around in the backyard, having an all-out war with water guns. It was the end of February, still cold but sunny. I sat on a lawn chair, pulled up the collar of my leather jacket, and watched as the "thugs" ran around, wreaking havoc. At one point, Pac grabbed a water gun and joined the fight. When he did this, I wanted to join in. I wanted a chance to break the ice and, also, it simply looked like fun. Just as I was thinking about joining in, Tupac put his gun down on the table next to me and got on the phone with Suge Knight. I waited about ten minutes to see if Pac would come back, but when he didn't, I picked up and examined the gun, wanting to be noticed by the others. They took the bait. Before I knew it, Mutah (a.k.a. Napoleon) of the Outlawz started squirting me with water. I jumped up and squirted him back. Within seconds, all the Outlawz surrounded me from every direction and started to spray me. I would not surrender as I continued my feeble attempt to soak them. Tupac ran into the middle, pushing them aside. "Now, that's what I'm talking about," said Pac. "You motherfuckers surrounded him, outnumbered him, but he still didn't give up. This is one crazy Iranian." From that day, "Crazy Iranian" became my nickname.

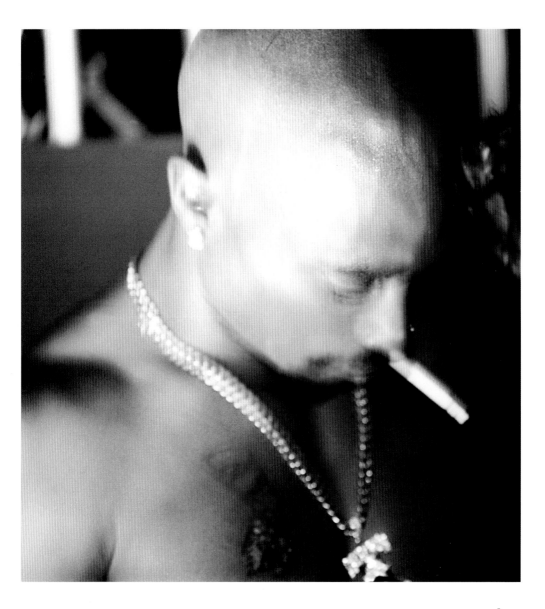

Tupac was an old soul. Meeting him for the first time felt familiar, as if I had known him in a previous incarnation. Class or status didn't matter to him. He was accepting and gave everyone acknowledgment. I felt his prophetic energy and wanted to protect him however I could. I wanted to be like an older brother who could help him fend off some of the drama that surrounded him.

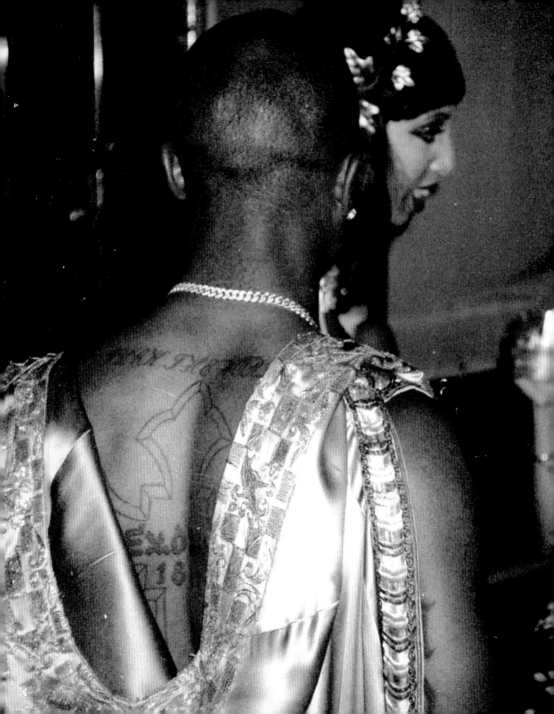

In November 1994, I was in Los Angeles when a phone call from New York delivered the information to Tracy Robinson that Tupac had been shot outside a studio and was dead. Tracy burst into tears. This was the first time (and, sadly, not the last) that I had seen violence bring sadness into Tracy's life. The next day, we found out that he was going to be okay and that he had already checked out of the hospital. He had been shot five times and insisted on leaving the hospital. Later, one of his friends told me that Tupac feared the shooters would try to finish the job. Years later, I discovered that he had checked out of the hospital and gone straight to the apartment of an actress friend of his. He stayed at her apartment for a month, surrounded by his group the Outlawz (his circle of faithful soldiers) and his beloved family, undetected.

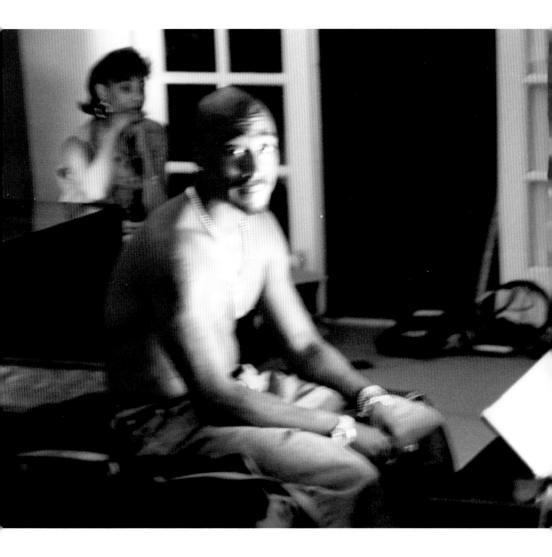

In 1995, Tracy and I drove from New York City to the massive cement structure upstate known as the Clinton Correctional Facility (in Dannemora), to visit Tupac in prison. I wanted to see him, but Tracy thought it best if I did not, as it had been some time since she had seen him and didn't know what to expect. I remember sitting in the car and thinking, Wow, Tupac Shakur is caged behind those walls.

Once I witnessed Tupac's character, I found it hard to believe the "rape" charges against him. Tupac never had to force himself on anyone. I often think Tupac would still be alive if he had not been incarcerated.

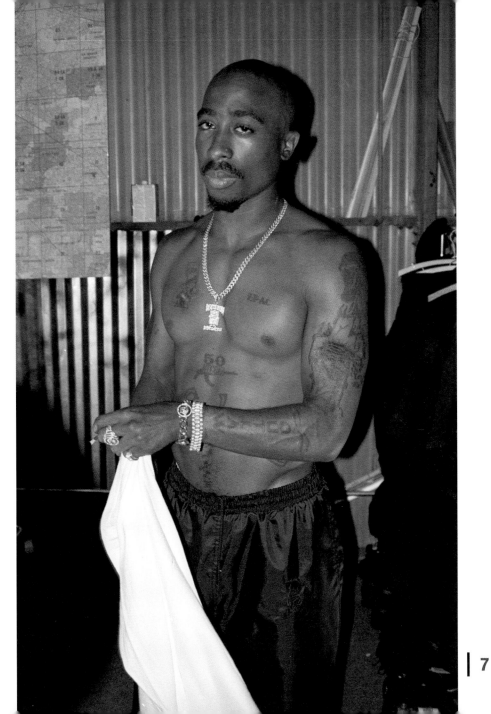

Tracy was working in production when she met Tupac. They had experienced an instant connection that eventually grew into a trusting friendship. Like so many others, Tracy was drawn to Tupac's shining energy and profound capacity to inspire others. Tracy says that when she looked at Tupac, it often seemed like he was glowing.

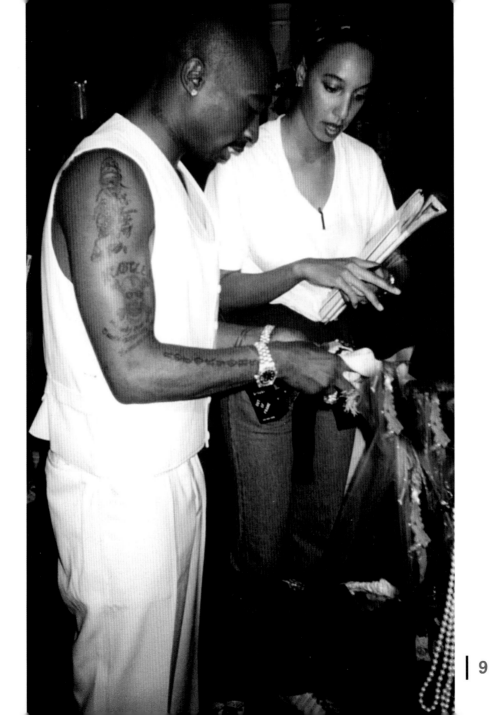

Other than the Outlawz and myself, Tupac's core support system consisted of women who had strong personalities. His mother, Afeni Shakur, was the foundation of that system. Yaasmyn Fula (mother of the Outlawz' Yafeu, or Kadafi), was Tupac's office manager and assistant, in addition to Molly Monjauze. Yaasmyn brought Tupac a trust and familiarity, while Molly was a loyal friend on whom he could rely.

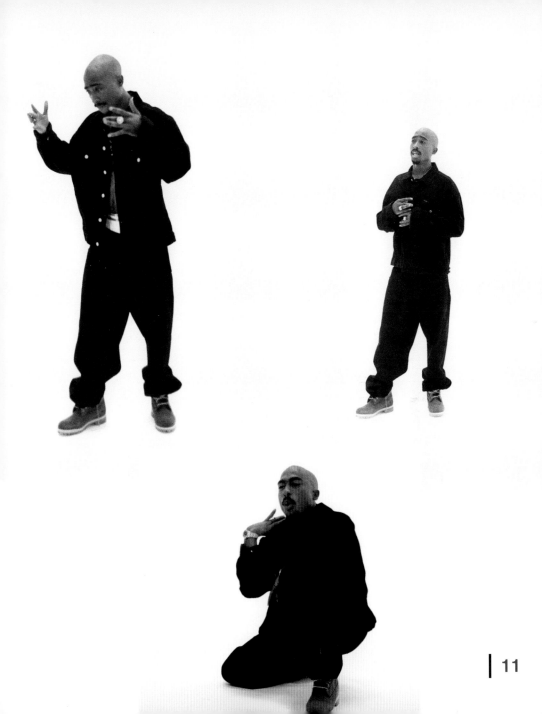

Tupac had enormous respect and admiration for all women, but especially black women. He took pride in helping women achieve their professional ambitions. His upbringing—growing up surrounded by a sister, aunts, female cousins, and his powerful mother, Afeni—kept him in tune with the struggles that women face.

He put Tracy in a powerful position and gave her a chance to shine in the male-dominated world of music-video production. Above all, Tracy had Tupac's trust, something he did not give out freely. Shortly before his death, he talked with Tracy and me about his plans to bring his ideas to the big screen.

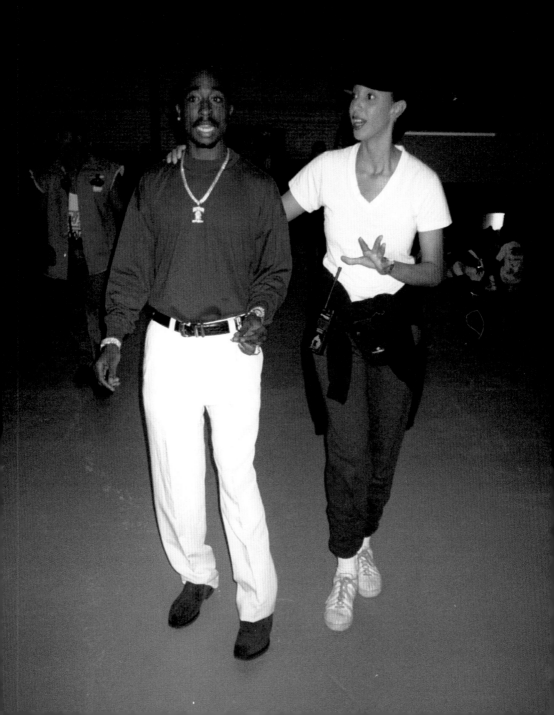

It was hard not to be charmed by Tupac. I wasn't simply a fan; I was a loyal business associate and friend as well. Although I wasn't sure what his fate would be, I knew beyond a doubt that his life would definitely have an impact on urban and American pop culture. As a director, I've spent time with a lot of celebrities, but I have yet to encounter anyone with his aura. There was something mystical and universal about him. He was more than a black man or an American; he was prophetic.

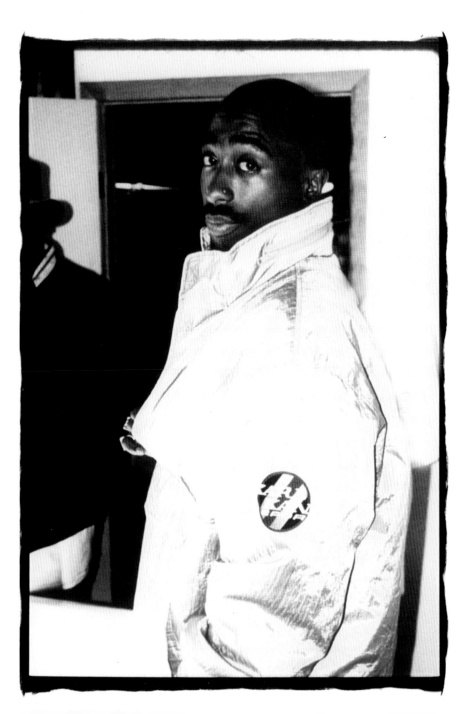

A common sight: Tupac laying down the law with a blunt in his hand.

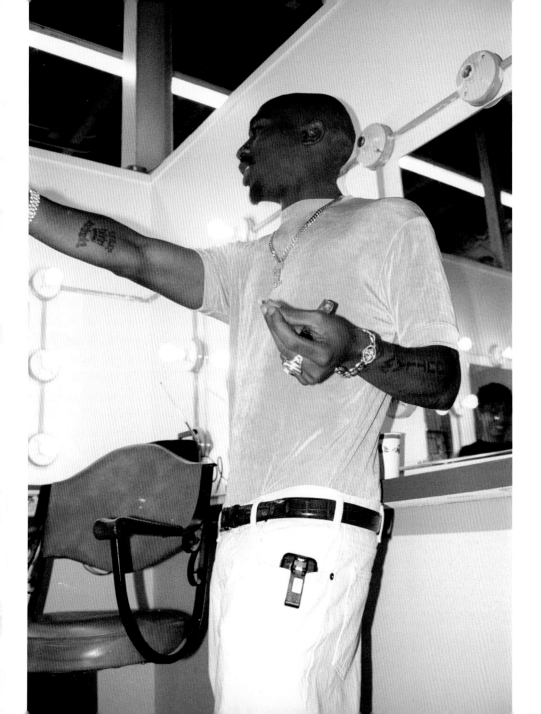

Tupac had more self-confidence than anyone I had ever met. The confident energy he projected compelled everyone around him to want to please him.

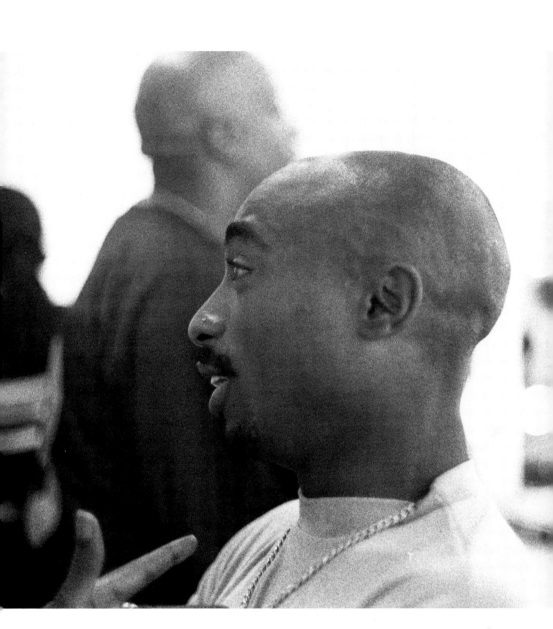

When Tupac performed, he was like a shaman in a trance. He was dynamic. It was as if he were channeling some sort of universal energy. It was this ability that fueled his group the Outlawz.

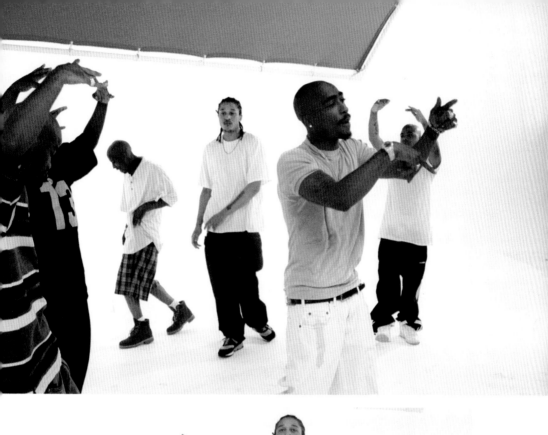

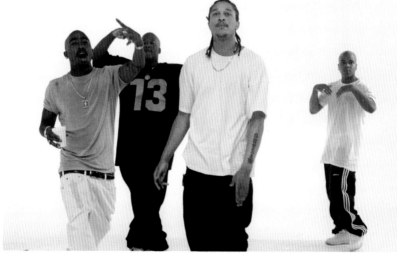

When Tupac signed to Death Row, he was put on an intense production schedule. We shot six big-budget music videos in just a few months, an unheard-of pace. I was puzzled and intrigued by how much this man could accomplish in such a small amount of time. There was a sense of urgency in everything he did. More than anything, I think he wanted to complete the terms of his record contract so he could be autonomous. He was ready to take on both the film and music industries in a big way. In 1996, Tupac created the film company 24/7 with Tracy and me, and the production company Euphanasia. Tupac devised the name by combining *euphoria* and *euthanasia*.

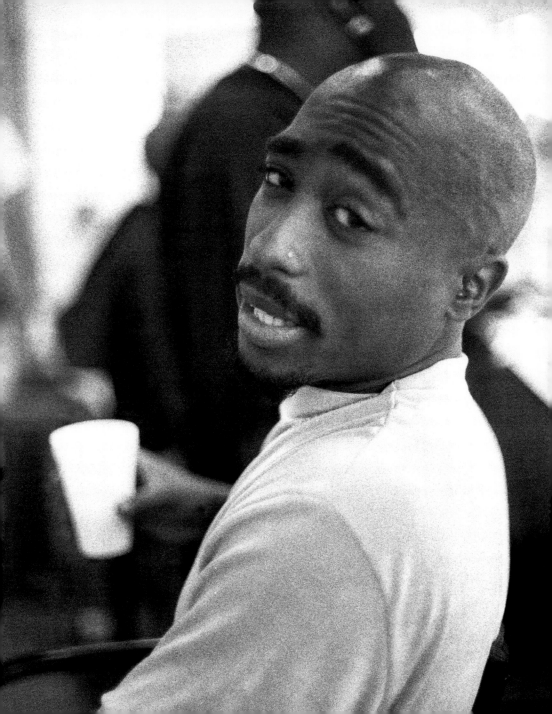

Once the camera started rolling, he was "on" without any reservation or trepidation. His performances always seemed so real because he was a master at creatively channeling all the positive and negative experiences of his life into what he was doing at the moment. The camera loved Pac.

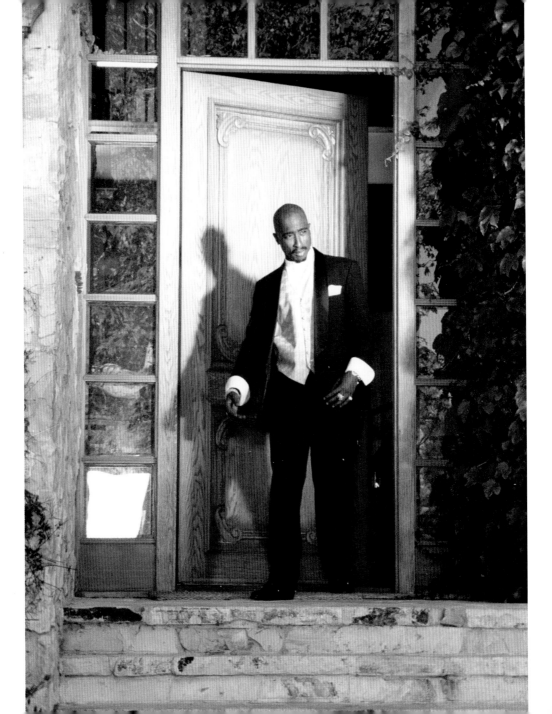

Pac's thug image faded away when he donned a suit. He looked like a prince or a dignitary. He was an innovator and worked hard at portraying himself in an unexpected fashion. Two years after Tupac's death, I started a production company, naming it Urban Warrior Films in his honor. Tupac was an urban warrior and inspired us to be the most we could be.

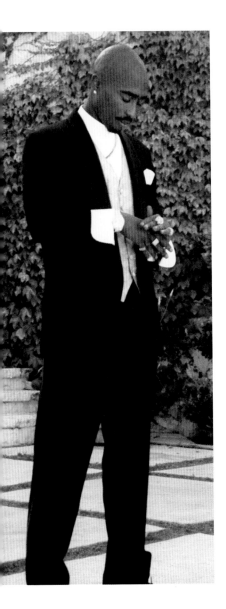

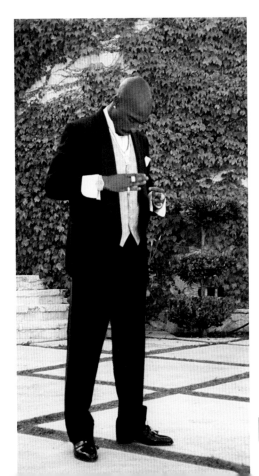

Other than his family, there were only a few people Tupac trusted. Like a general, he had his own small army, which were called the Outlawz. The Outlawz were his group, his loyal soldiers, and his devoted disciples. Like him, most of them were children of Black Panthers or the offspring of the black struggle. A keeper of the Shakur legacy, Tupac honored the soldiers whose lives touched his and whose sacrifices shaped his belief.

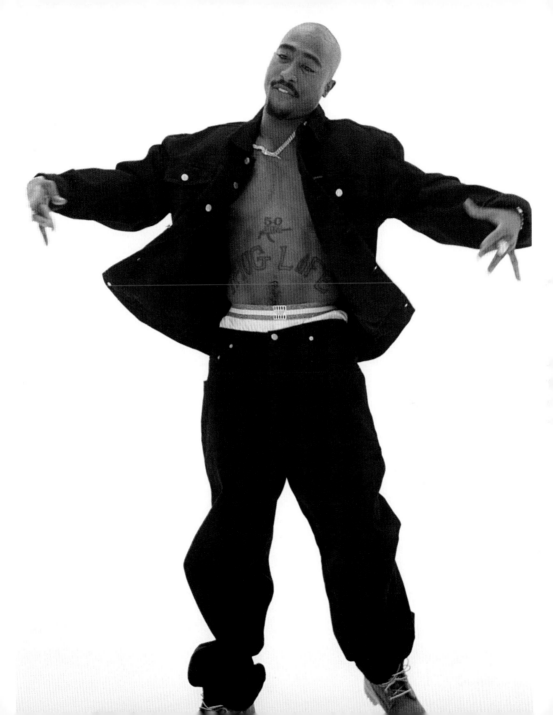

The fun thing about working with Pac was that he was always ready to do something completely unexpected of a rapper. When they made the music video "All About U," Tracy and a few of the other women on the production crew donned Egyptian garb to cut down on the overtime cost of hiring professional models.

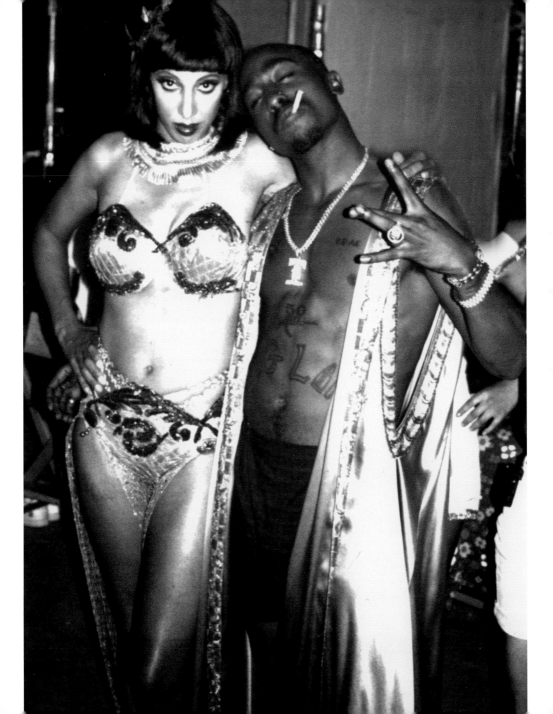

Tupac's million-dollar smile. Women used to throw themselves at him. They would do anything just to get close to him, which further negates any notion that Tupac would ever take advantage of a woman. Men envied or resented him because of how inadequate they felt around him.

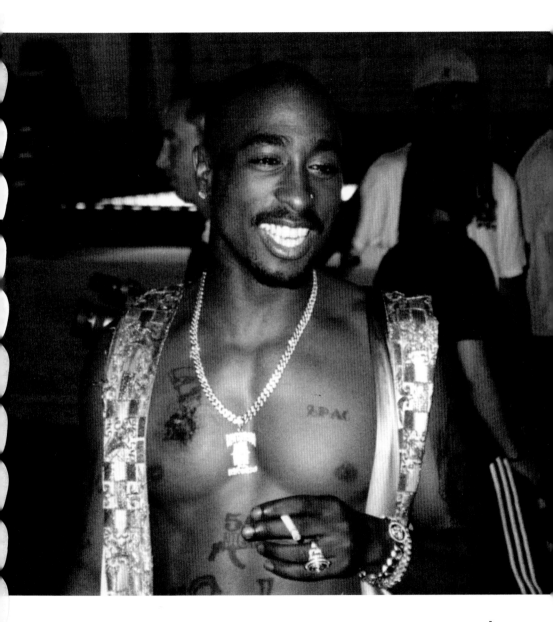

Whether he performed on camera or in front of a crowd, you couldn't take your eyes off him. He exploded into performance.

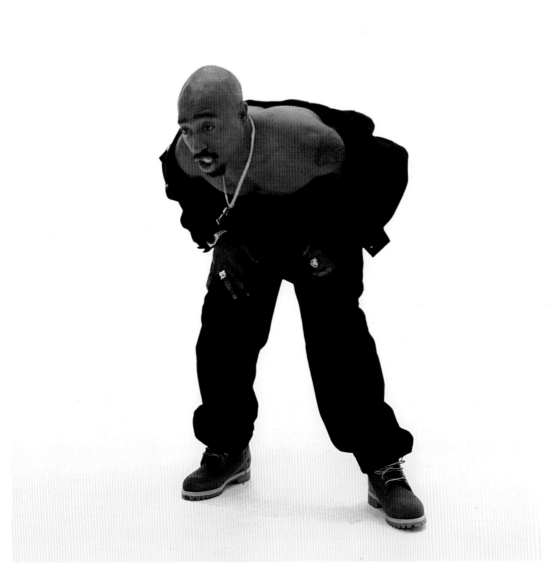

Tracy and I were producing a video titled "2 of Amerikaz Most Wanted," which featured Tupac and Snoop Dogg. The scheduled director called two days prior to the shoot and announced that he did not want to direct the video because he didn't want to share credit with the artist, even if the video's concept had been Tupac's idea. Tracy, knowing my desire to direct, suggested I codirect with Tupac, whose response was, "Let the muthafucka do it."

My first directing experience, "2 of Amerikaz Most Wanted," became one of the most heavily rotated videos in MTV history.

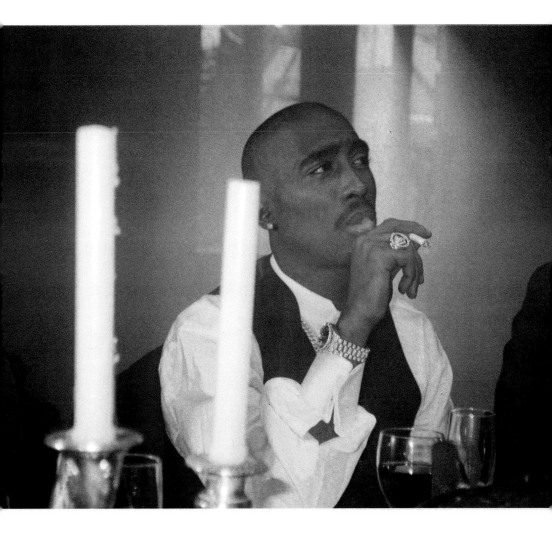

This picture is a good example of how Tupac's mood would change at the drop of a hat. This is Tupac between takes, in a typically pensive state.

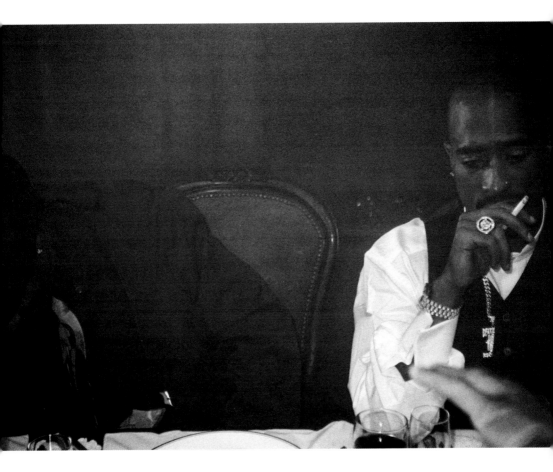

Here I am explaining how I intended to shoot the next setup.

Tupac was eager to get a couple of his own film productions going. To get the ball rolling, he came up with an idea for "Made Niggaz," a short film with all the elements of a narrative story line and three music videos feathered throughout.

Tupac's refusal to accept anything other than one's best effort forced everyone on the crew (from production assistant to director of photography) to work as hard as possible.

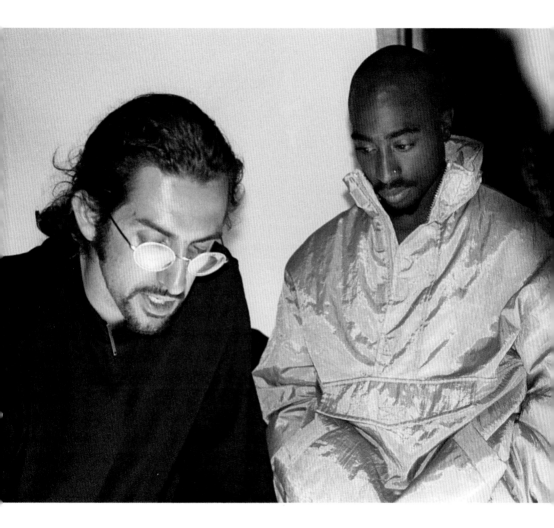

One of the biggest challenges of directing and producing music videos for Tupac was keeping everyone on his typically ambitious schedule.

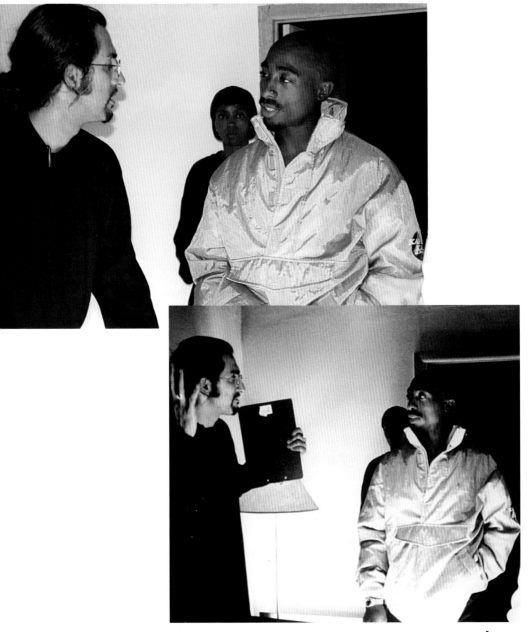

Waiting for the next setup, Tupac was always busy either checking out the next shot or doing business on the phone.

Tupac was always ready to push the envelope. Whenever he came up with a theme or an idea for the next job, Tracy and I would drop everything and get on it.

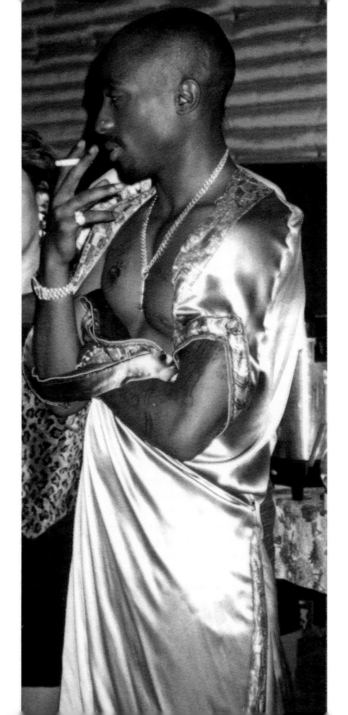

He never stopped moving. Between takes, I invariably wondered what Tupac was thinking. It always seemed as though he was pondering his next move in life and how to handle the obstacles that lay before him.

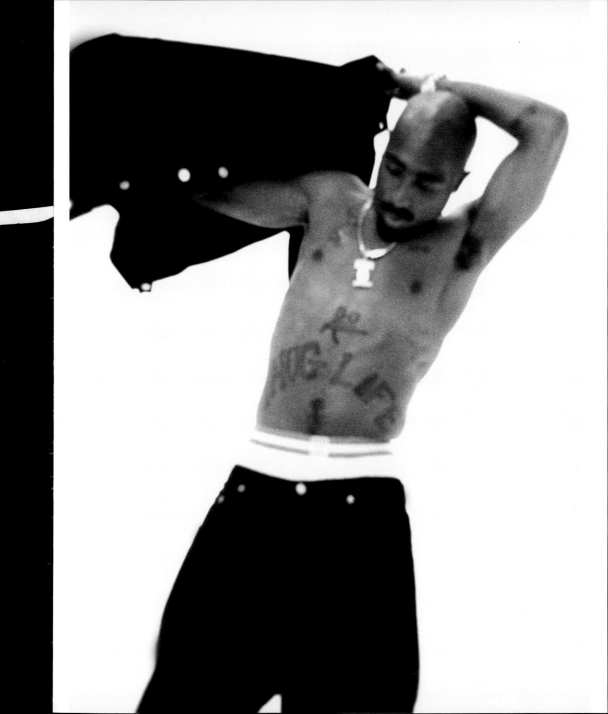

One night, Tracy and I were summoned to Tupac's apartment on Wilshire Boulevard. There, Tupac began to discuss plans to start a production company. A couple of studios were ready to offer him a multipicture deal. He had decided to make Tracy and me his partners, and we were absolutely ecstatic. When I suggested 24/7 productions as the name of the company, he loved it. We were going to shake up the industry with 24/7.

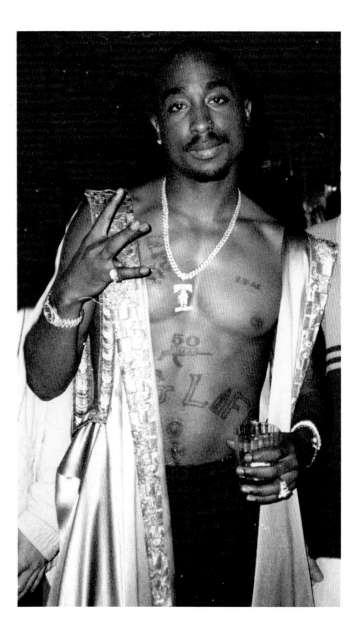

One important facet of Tupac's personality was his sense of humor. Although he was serious most of the time, he often took time out to make fun of himself and others. This is a picture of Tupac impersonating Rick James. We shot video footage of Tupac performing his own version of "Super Freak." I had the pleasure of working with Rick James in 1998 and showed him the footage. Rick practically fell on the floor, laughing. After he composed himself, he mocked, "If that nigga was alive, I'd kick his ass."

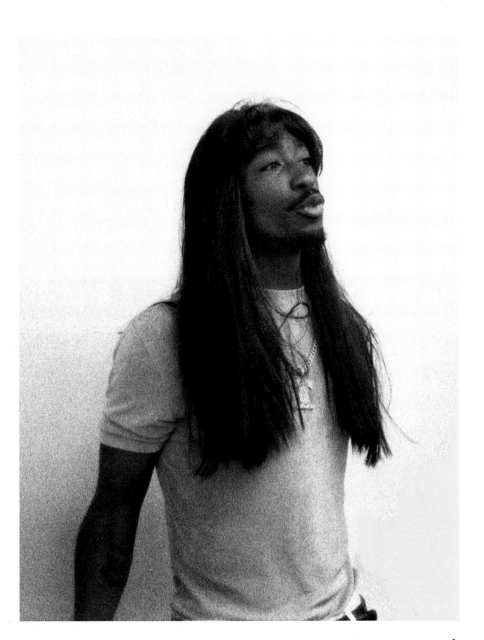

Tupac had an intensity that I had never seen in anyone, yet every so often I would see a hint of sadness in his demeanor.

Whether shooting a still photograph or a video, being like a fly on the wall afforded me a candid look at Tupac with his guard down. Although he surrounded himself with people, at times he seemed to be very alone.

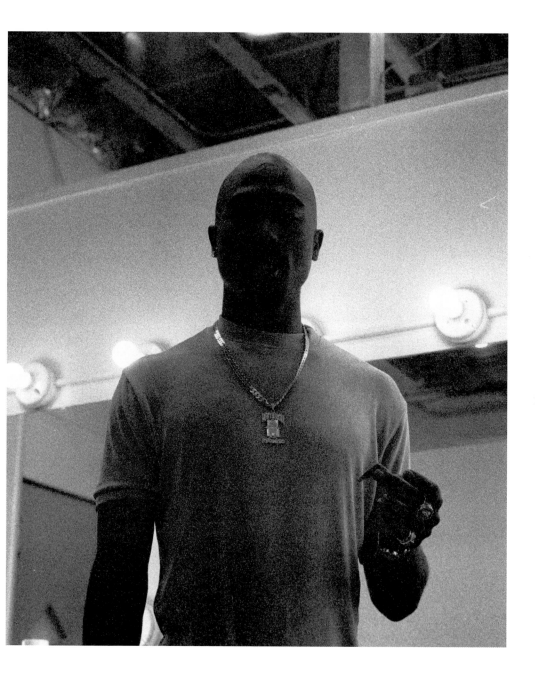

There are many photographs of Tupac in which he looks down or to the side, as if in deep thought. He had his hands full supporting a large family and dealing with the dark forces that surrounded him. Ironically, when he smiled, I couldn't avoid noticing a profound sense of sadness just underneath his sparkling eyes.

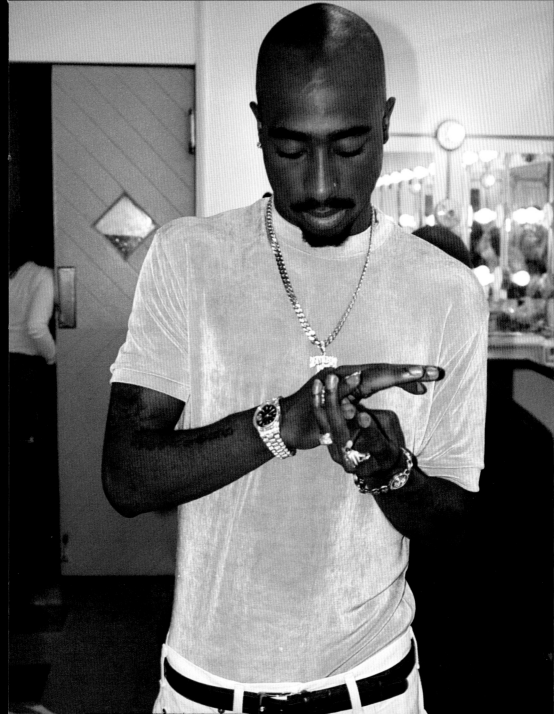

A powerful rage fueled Pac's energetic performances. I've worked with a lot of artists since his passing but have yet to experience anyone with his type of energy in front of the camera.

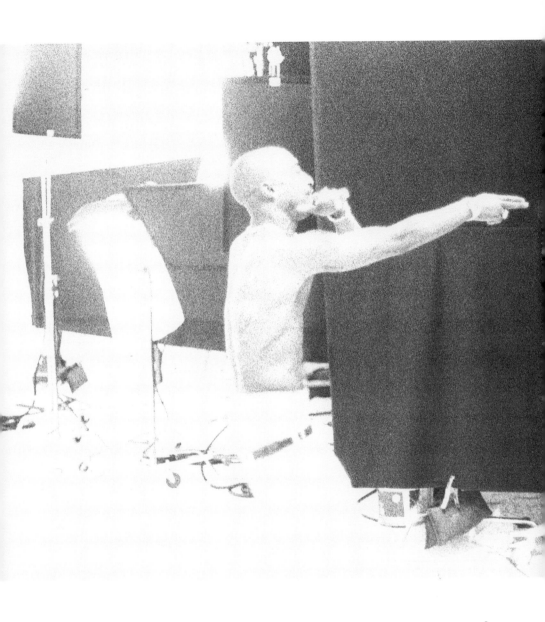

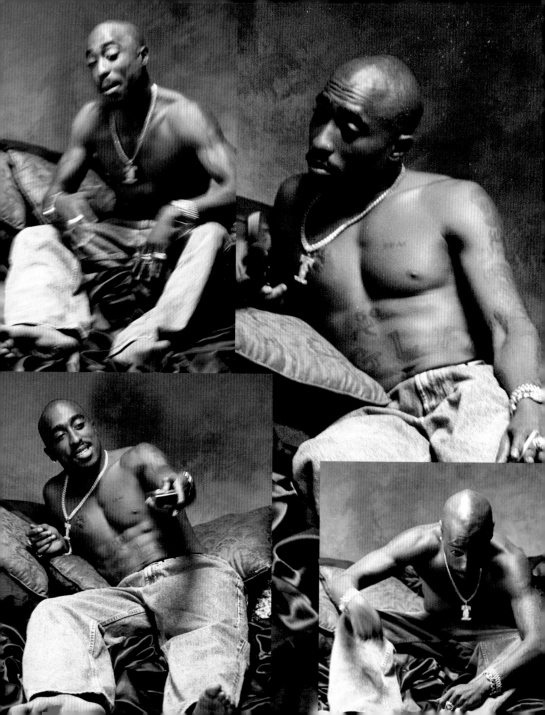

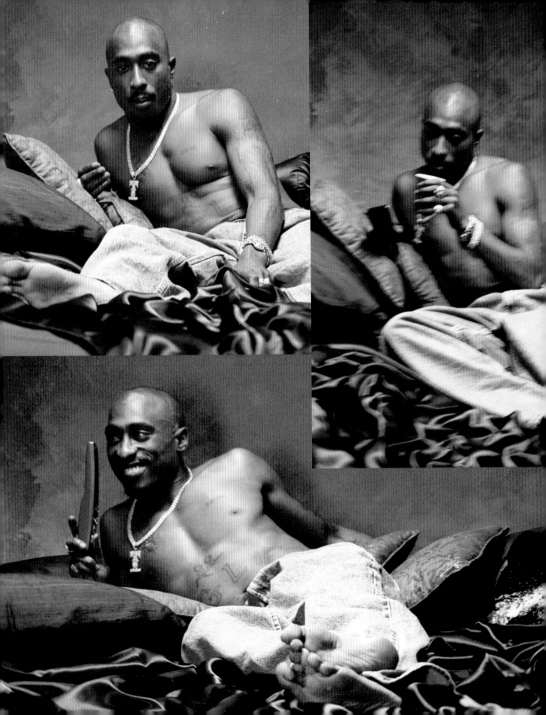

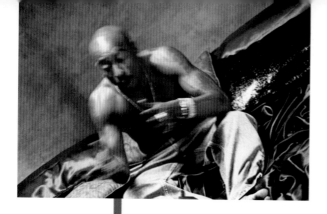

Tupac was a true Gemini. Being in his presence on a daily basis allowed me to see many sides of him. He was at once a very serious, uncompromising workaholic who expected everyone to stay up (literally—Tupac could work twenty-two hours a day). Pac was also accepting, loving, hilarious, and comedic and a true lover of life who relished new experiences. He symbolized innovation and moved at lightning speed. He put everyone to the test. He pushed the Outlawz on the flow and speed of their delivery. He also pushed my crew when I produced or directed a music video for him. He was a good human being evolving into a stellar one.

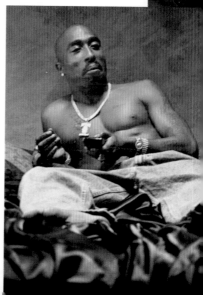

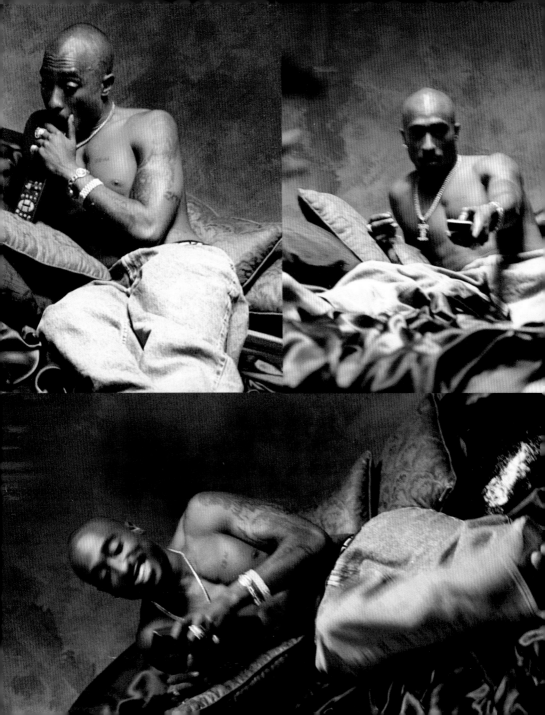

Tupac's name means "shining serpent." *The Art of War* by Sun-tzu, one of Tupac's favorite books, teaches you to keep your friends close and your enemies closer so that you can be aware of their actions.

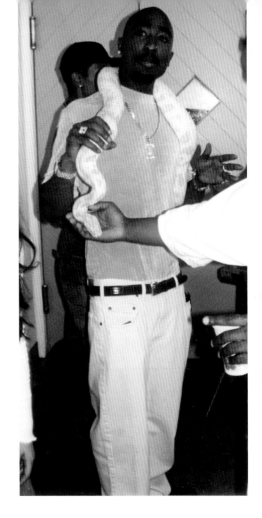
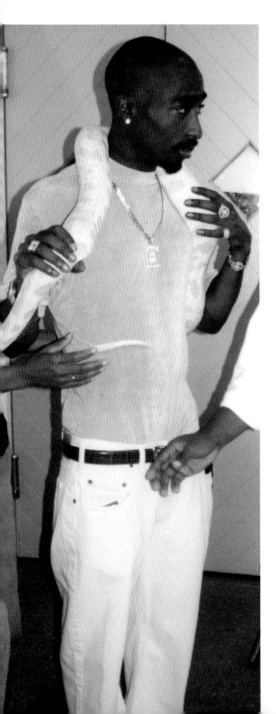

Each anniversary of Tupac's passing is difficult for his family and friends. Either on or near the day of his passing, I always seem to remember the craziest things happening around the world.

I remember, on one particular anniversary, reading about the time a Peruvian rebel group called Tupac Amarú had stormed a government building in Lima and taken hostages.

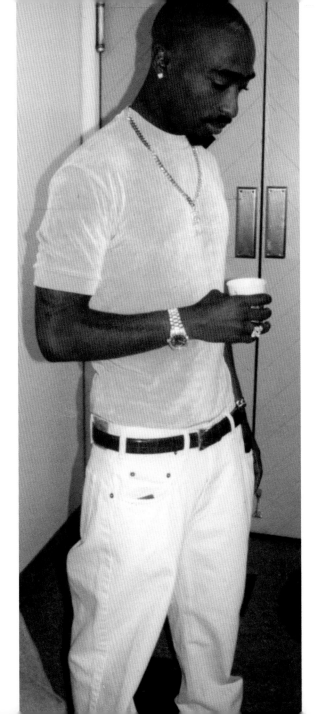

Tupac would shoot a movie during the day, a video at night, and, if he had any extra time in a twenty-four-hour period, he would make his way to the studio and drop a couple of tracks. If he could, he'd sleep in the limo between locations. If Tupac was able to sleep in his own bed, then Molly had the duty of waking him in the morning. We used to hear all kinds of "Tupac not wanting to be woken up" stories. We learned early on that waking Tupac in the morning was a thankless job.

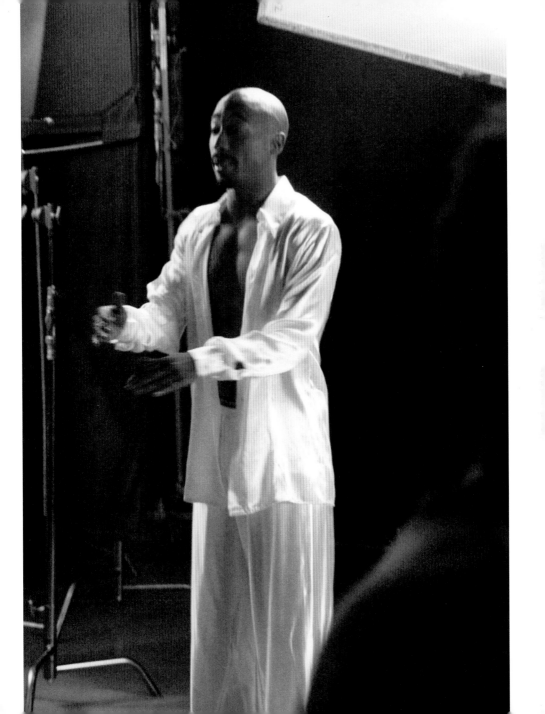

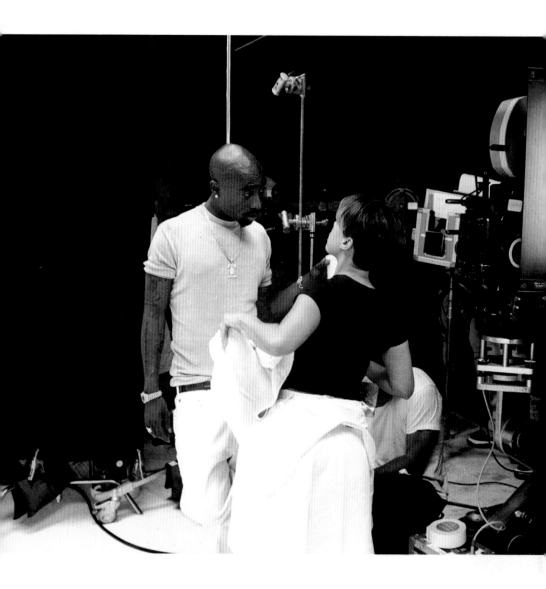

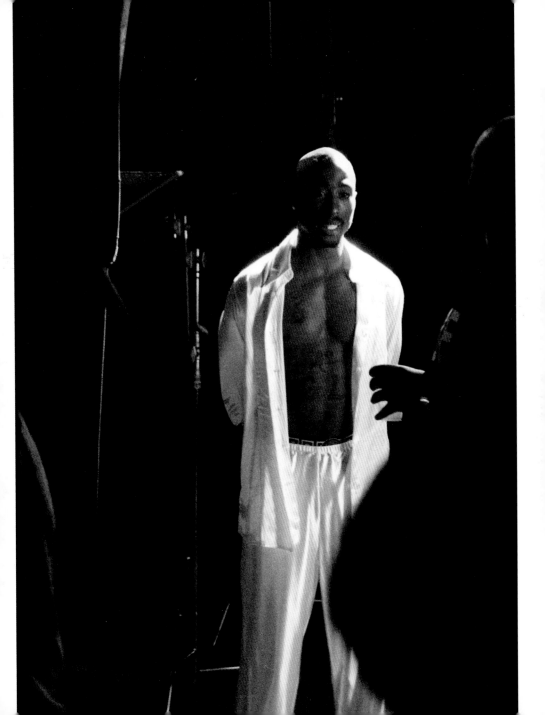

Tupac was a true perfectionist. He enjoyed things of superior quality. He made sure that every representation of himself was of the highest caliber.

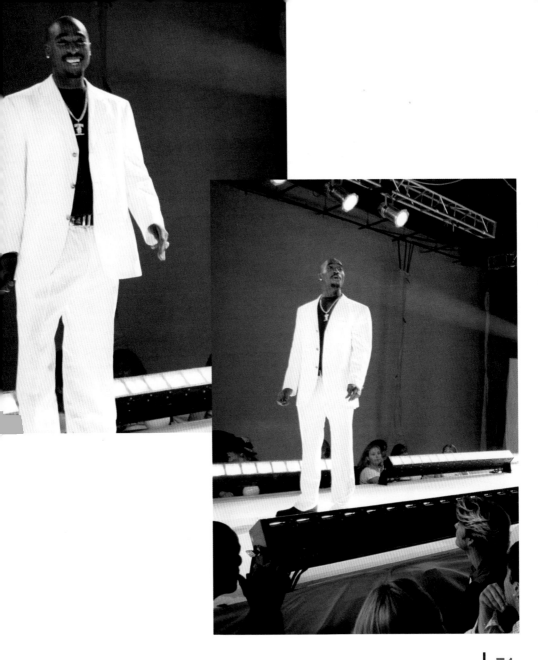

The environment in which Tupac lived and worked was nothing less than intense. Being with him in that environment made me think that God had placed me there for a reason, and my relationship with Tupac began to take precedence over my other relationships. I know I was someone on whom he could depend. At times I felt as though we were a strong yet vulnerable team—one moment conquering the world, the next being swept up in a tornado that was looming on the horizon. The intense eight months I spent as one of his partners were some of the most rewarding yet frightening months of my life.

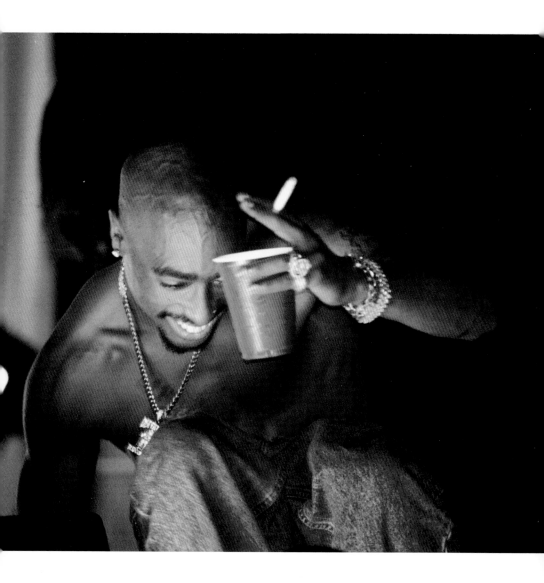

Pac flashing the infamous "Westside" sign. He would say that no matter what city he lived in, he always seemed to end up on the Westside. He had lived in New York, Baltimore, Oakland, Marin City, California, and Los Angeles.

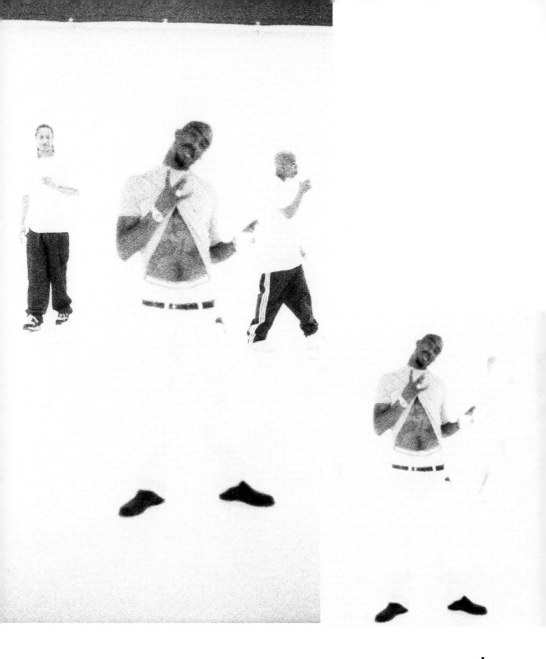

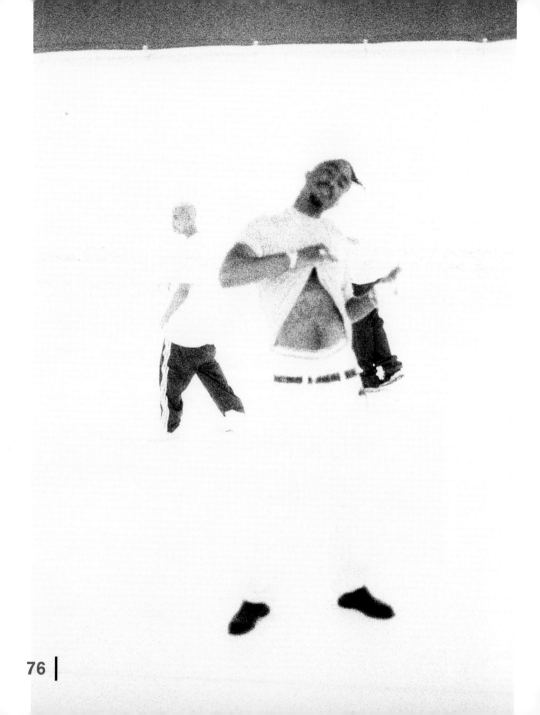

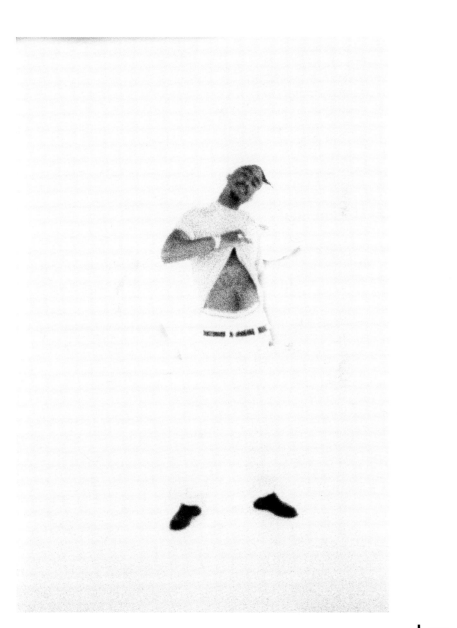

When it came to production, Tupac always had a clear vision of what he wanted to achieve. He knew exactly what he wanted, and he demanded pure dedication. His favorite name for the inept was "goat-mouth muthafucka."

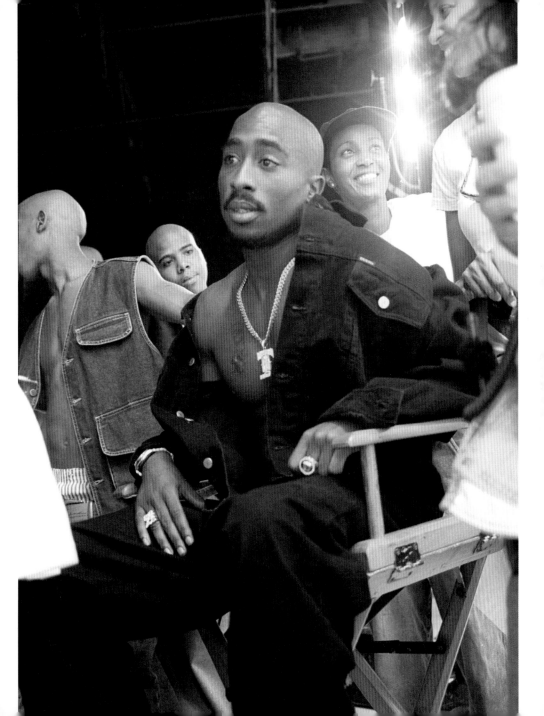

Tupac was notorious for his run-ins with the law, which motivated the use of police disguises in the "Made Niggaz" short. Unfortunately, this project never made it to fruition. Luckily, however, I was able to salvage a music video out of the footage.

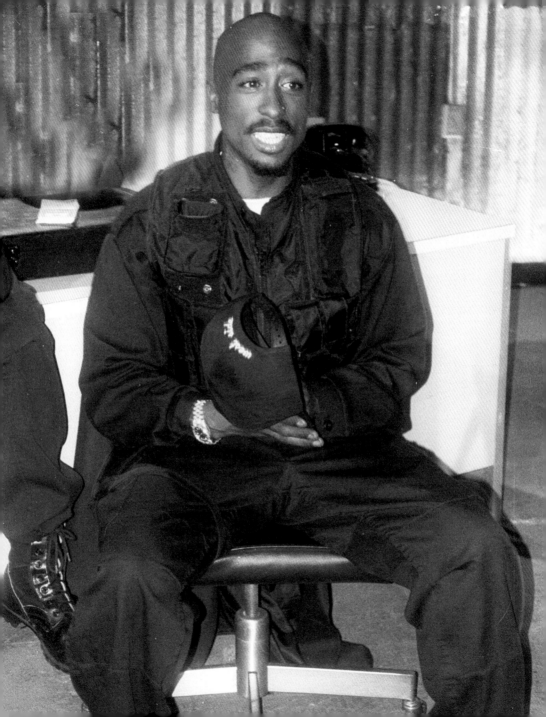

We had a large number of explosions and gunplay in the "Made Niggaz" scenes, which required various professionals (pyrotechnicians and visual-effects experts) to get the set ready. The excess time it took to get all the firepower ready frustrated the artists.

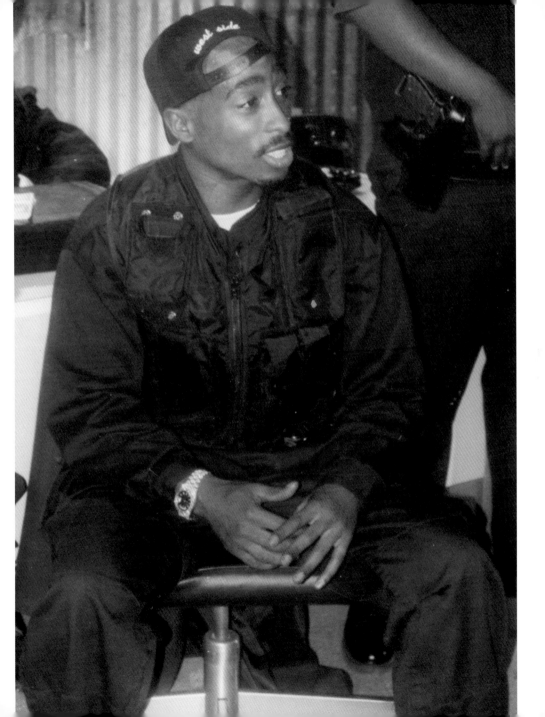

Tupac was a true professional and would deliver 100 percent of the time. Tupac would move, bounce around, and perform for the camera with unmatched fervor and energy.

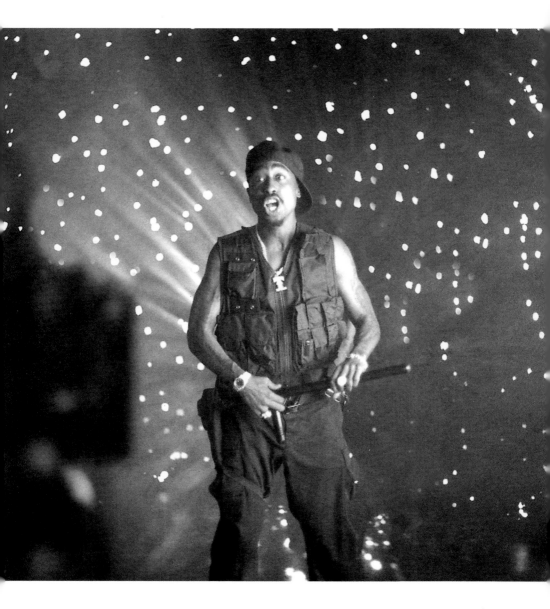

Tupac would want to shoot a four-day movie in eight hours. Most revolutionaries are constantly preoccupied with time: They know that tomorrow is not promised.

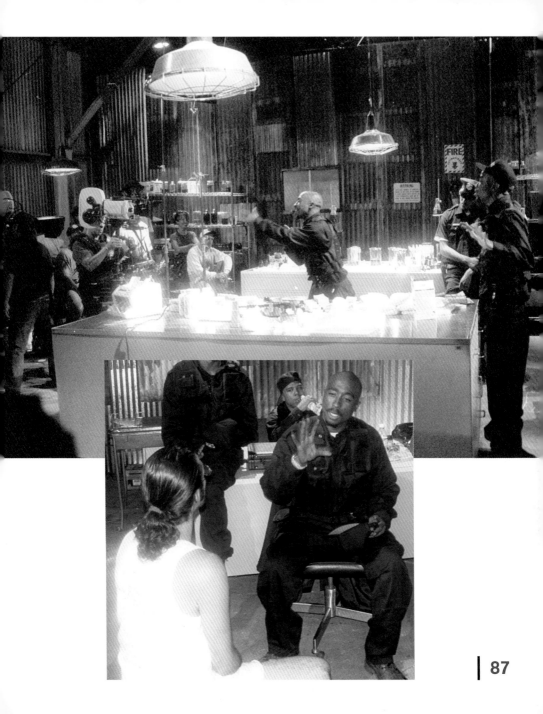

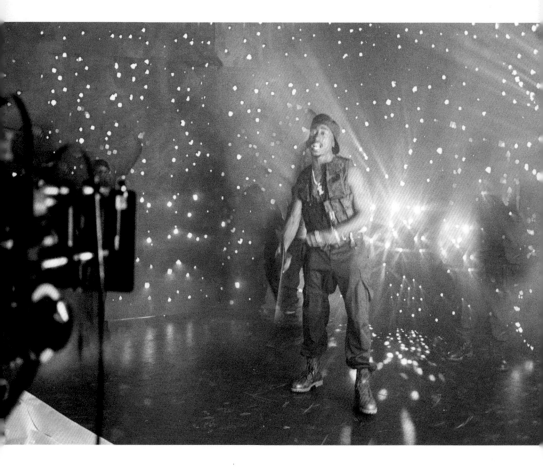

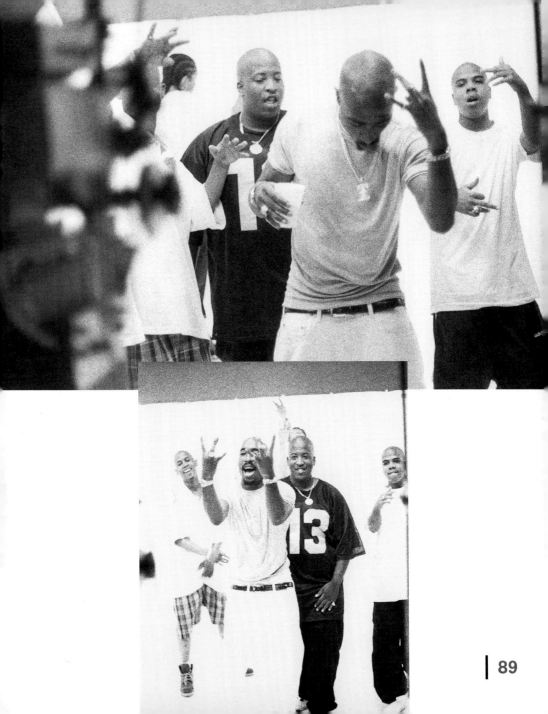

A perfect example of Tupac's seldom-exposed humorous side. Here he is demonstrating the proper way to cook pasta to an Italian chef!

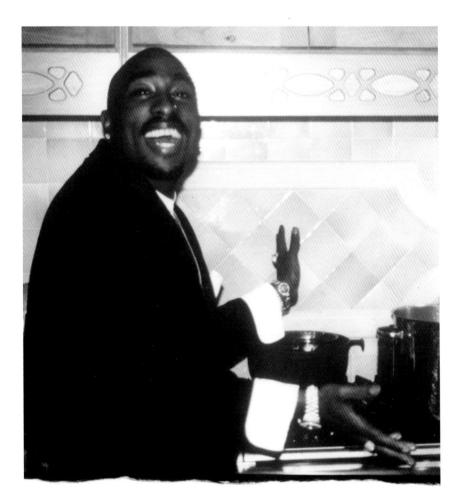

Yafeu ("Yaki") of the Outlawz was extremely close to Tupac. The two were like blood brothers. Yaki told people that he had witnessed Tupac's shooting. A few months after Pac's passing, a few of us went to Atlanta to work on a Tupac memorial for Afeni Shakur. The day after we completed filming the memorial, we received a call from Kidada Jones, who told us that Yaki had been shot. Molly rushed up to New Jersey and was by his side until his mother, Yaasmyn, arrived. Yaki passed away later that day. To this day, it's still hard to believe that neither Tupac nor Yaki is still alive.

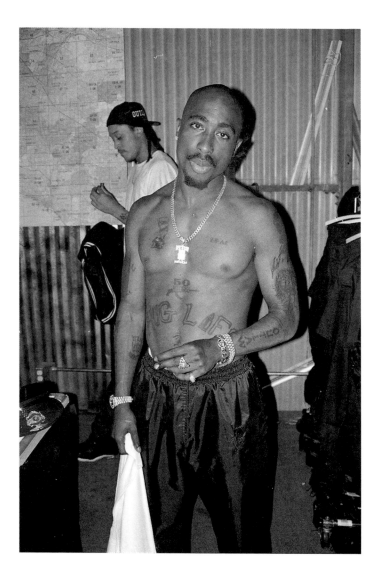

Dye Charles was Tupac's stylist and always had him looking dapper.

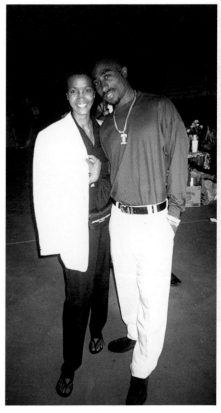

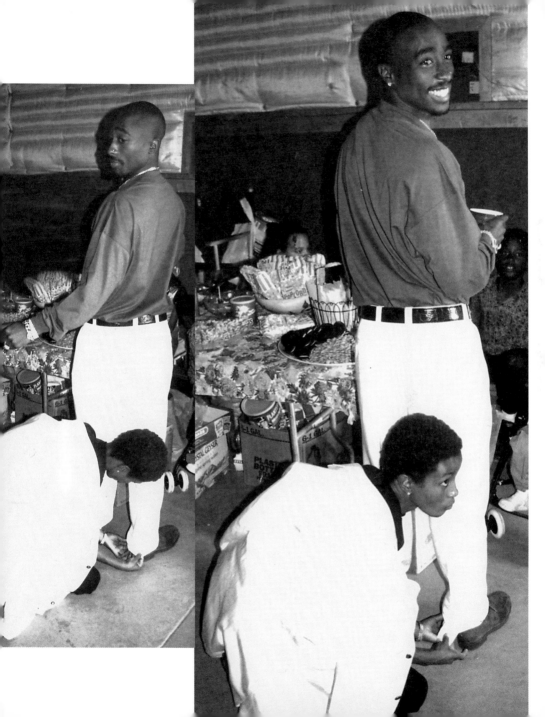

As a director, it was always a pleasure to work with Tupac.

He was always ready to try something new, different, and challenging. He had exquisite taste. If something made sense and felt good, then he tried it. His record company fought him regarding the concept for the "Pour Out a Little Liquor" video. The concept wasn't thug/street enough for them, and the label didn't like the idea of Tupac dressed in period clothing. Tupac did not relent. The label, however, would only agree to use the footage if Tupac ended the video with a contemporary thug-type scene. Needless to say, Tupac didn't show up for the extra shoot.

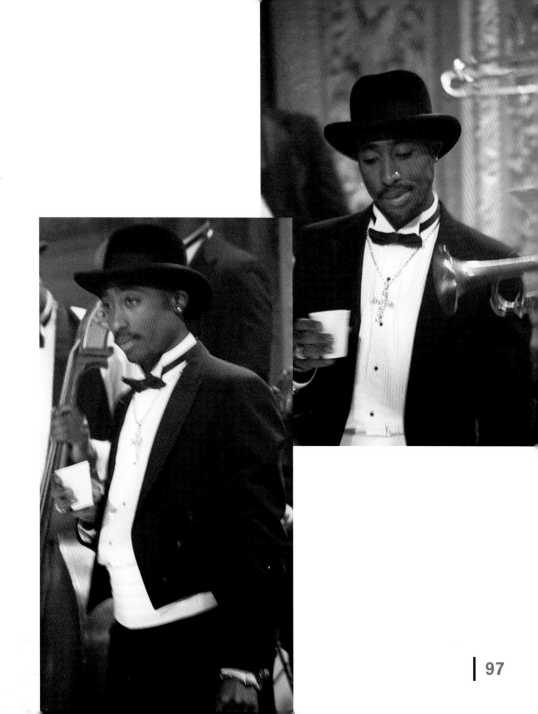

Tupac seemed happiest when he was on a set or in the studio. He was a powerful motivating force to everyone around him.

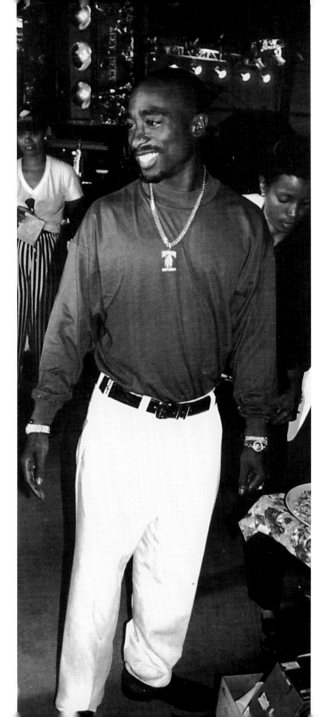

Tupac loved children. I think it was their innocence that attracted him. He was always innovative and unconventional. On the "All About U" video, he featured children who were chosen from a group of disadvantaged kids. After the shoot, Tupac anonymously paid for one of the girls to go to a dance academy.

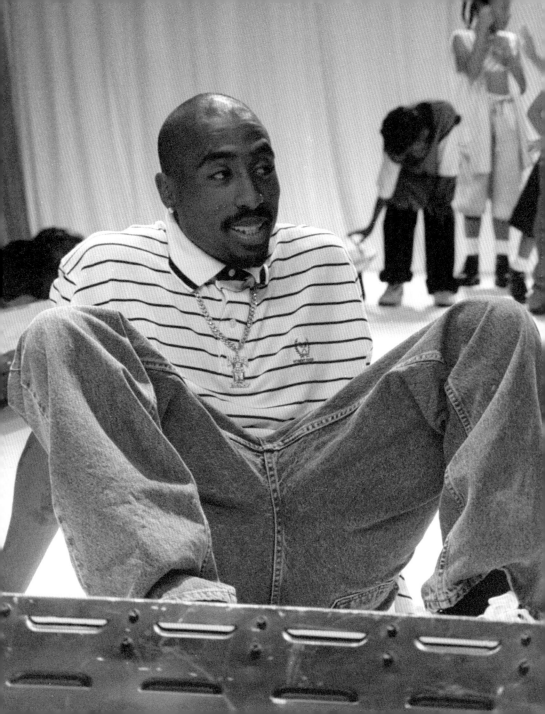

Tupac loved his fans. He always accommodated them. Even here, on the busy set of a video, he took time between takes to give his fans some love.

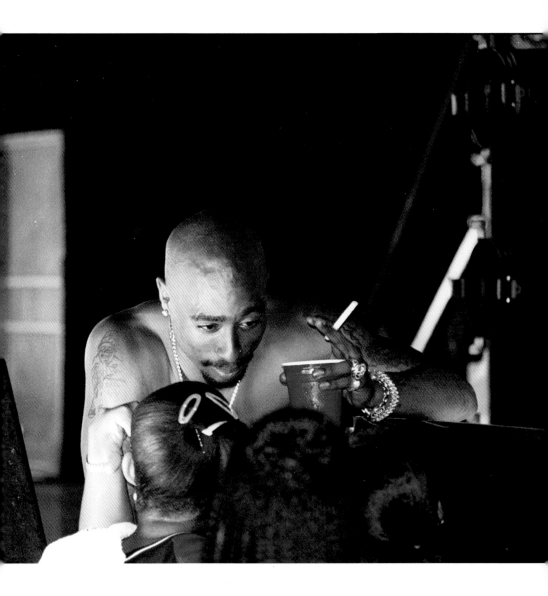

Tracy and I were producing PG- and R-rated versions of a video called "How Do U Want It," which had a lot of naked women running around on the set. Not wanting to make the girls uncomfortable, Pac asked the crew members to take off their shirts for the shoot. It was quite a sight, and allowed for everyone to drop his or her guard a bit.

After the shoot, Pac had a party at his hotel suite with the video's director and most of the female performers. That party was anything but a PG night!

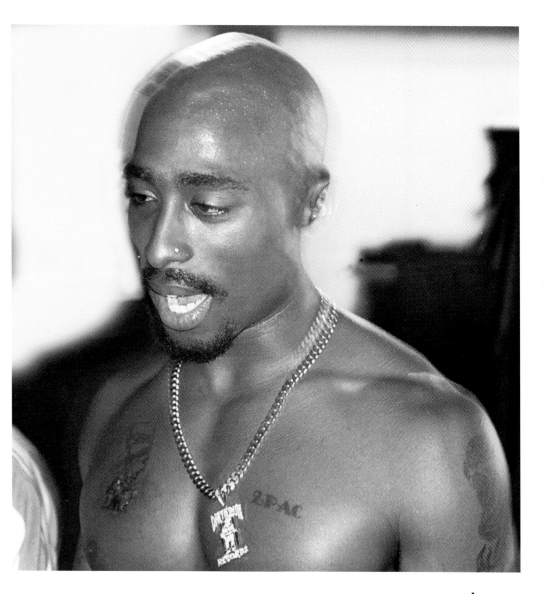

Just prior to his death, I was shooting a living documentary of Tupac. One night at his house in Calabasas, California, he said, "If the powers that be build a youth center for us in each and every ghetto in America, I'll kiss Biggie on the cheek and perform at each and every one of them for free."

It's interesting how the media has exposed only Tupac's negative aspects.

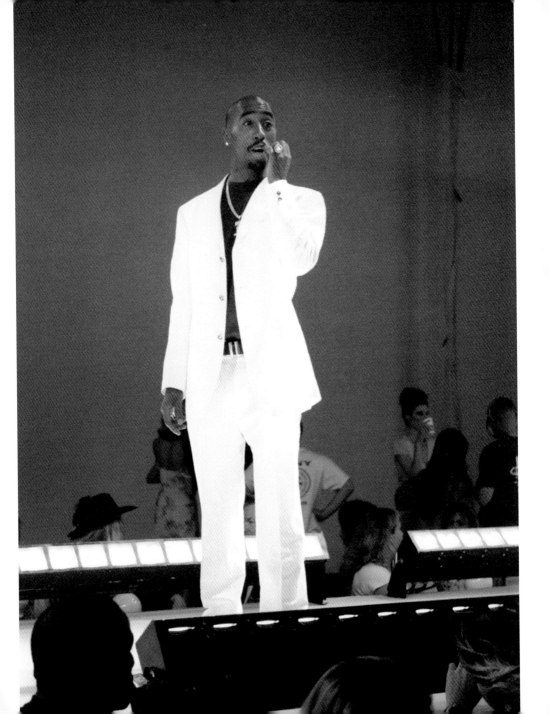

Tupac wearing his infamous Hush Puppies; we all had them in a variety of colors.

Tupac treated his music and film crews with a very high regard. I think that working on music-video and film sets over the years taught him an appreciation for the production process itself.

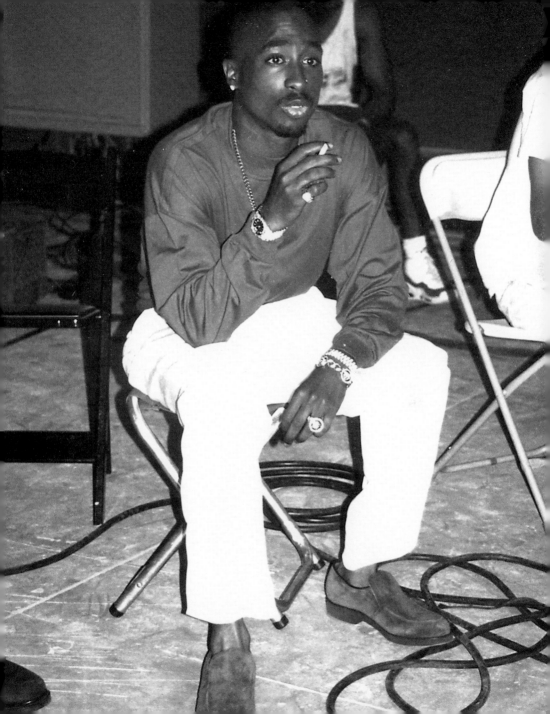

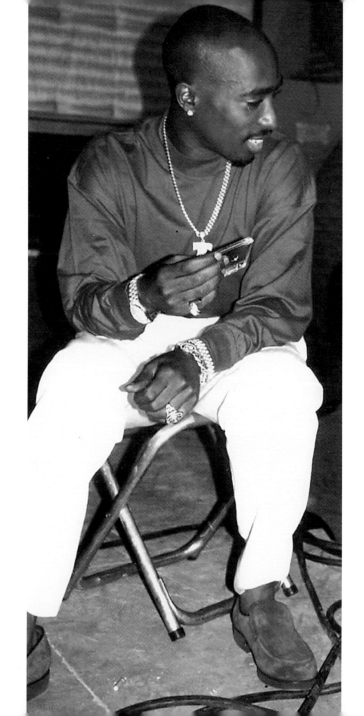

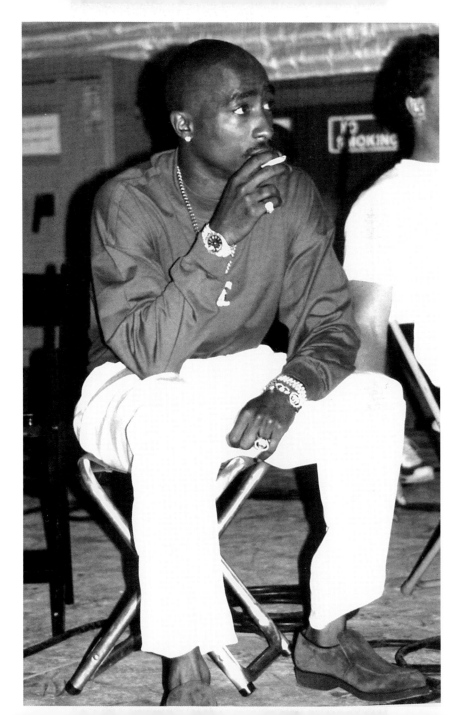

I bought this truck with the intention of tricking it out. Pac used it in a short film we were shooting. A week after he passed away, I was sideswiped and the truck was totaled.

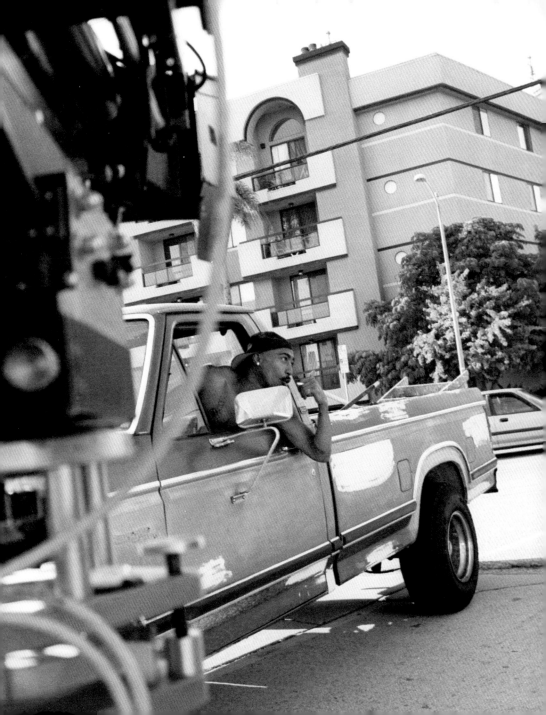

Tupac started to crave autonomy. He met with film studios and they said that they were willing to work with him on condition that he stay out of legal trouble (which he did).

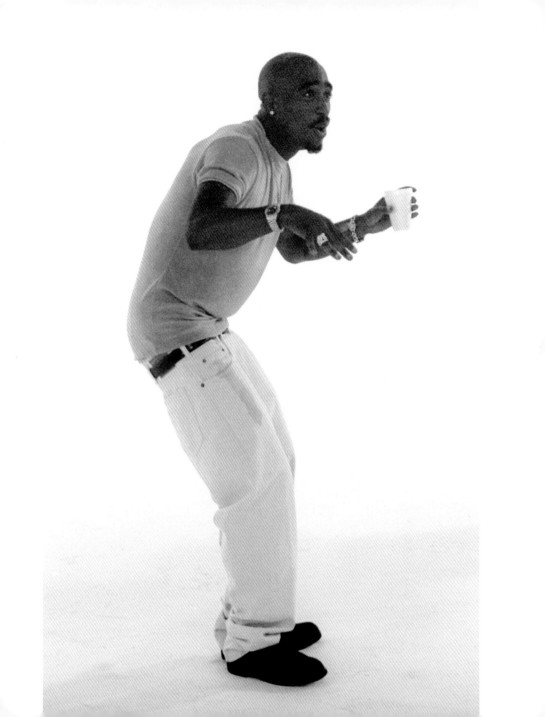

Despite his sometimes stressed surroundings, Tupac was able to kid around and have fun. Here he is giving makeup tips to one of the Outlawz, Fatal Hussein.

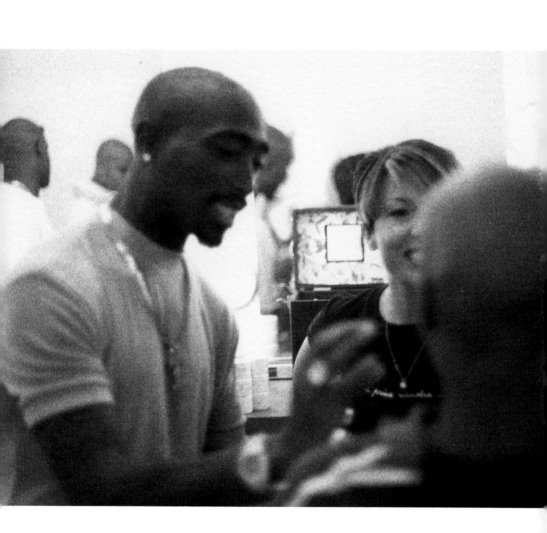

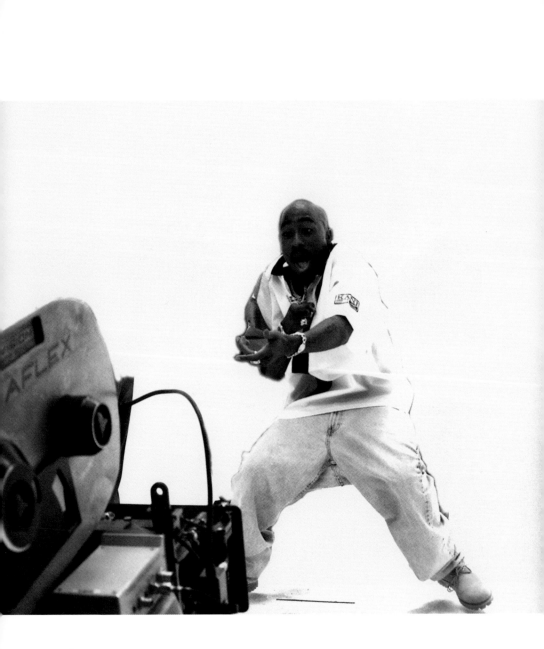

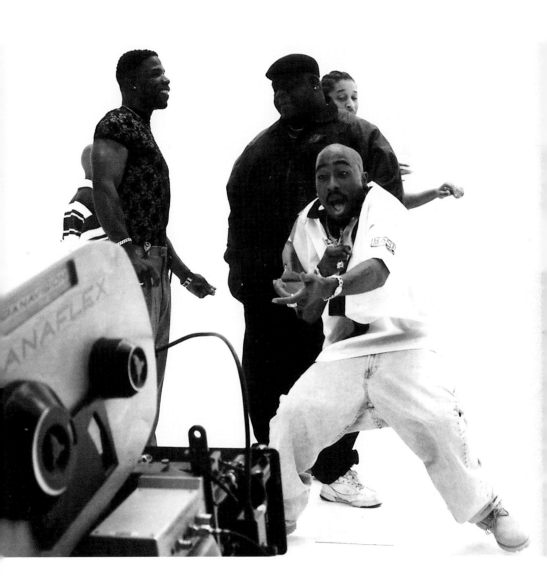

Tupac had serious issues with the whole Bad Boy camp. Although I wasn't privy to the intricacies of the situation, I knew that Tupac was a very loyal person. He was forthcoming and without a bullshit veneer. He approached the dissing he did in his videos with the scorn of betrayal.

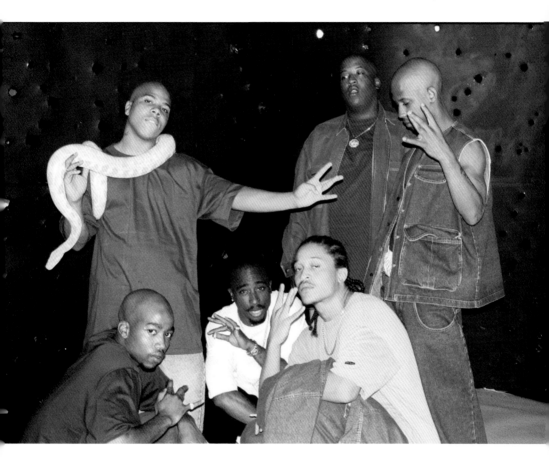

Eager to see the last setup and analyze his performance, Tupac attentively watched the playback monitor. If he wasn't happy with his performance, he would do it over.

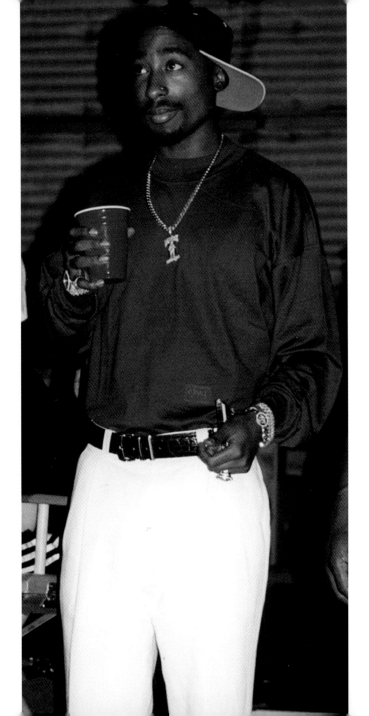

The media fanned the misconception that Tupac was a misogynist. That perception was far from the truth, and the Blocker sisters proved to be a perfect example: beautiful women who were simply friends.

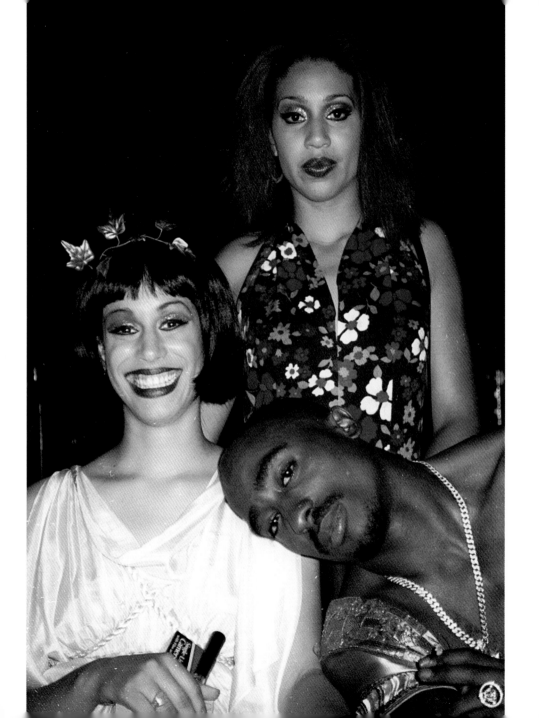

Tupac was on his way to Italy with his fiancée, Kidada Jones, to perform in a Versace fashion show. I pleaded with him to let me go so I could shoot stills and video, but he wouldn't let me. He said he wanted time alone with his lady. I later saw pictures of him looking very happy on the runway.

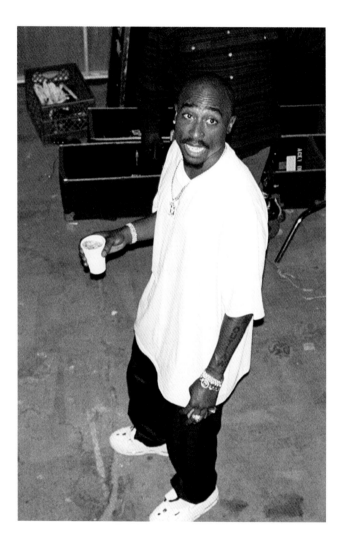

Tupac liked to wear SWAT gear. I think the number of times he was harassed by police contributed to the pleasure he received whenever he wore one of their uniforms. His band of Outlawz was always ready and willing to do whatever he wanted in the name of performance.

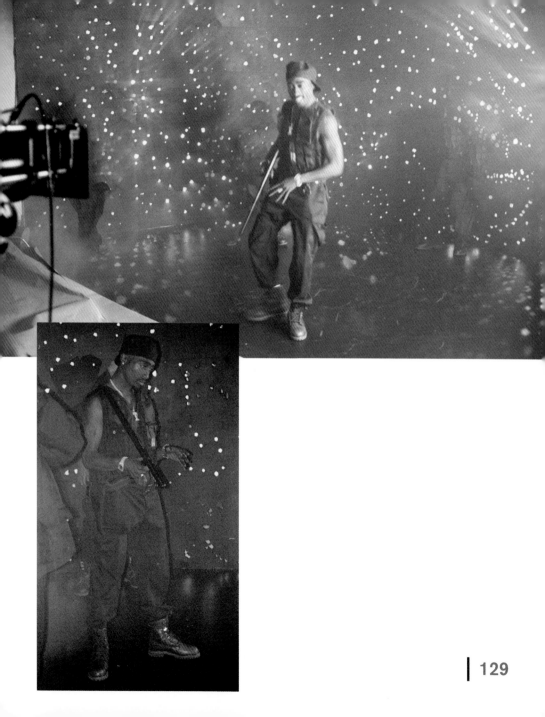

Tracy, Tupac, and music-video director Marlene Rhein.

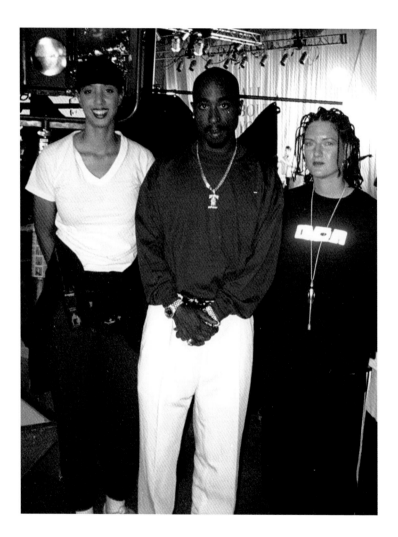

Tupac was the reason we were together; he was the reason for our activities and schedule. It's important for his fans to see these photos so that they can glimpse Pac in candid, unguarded settings.

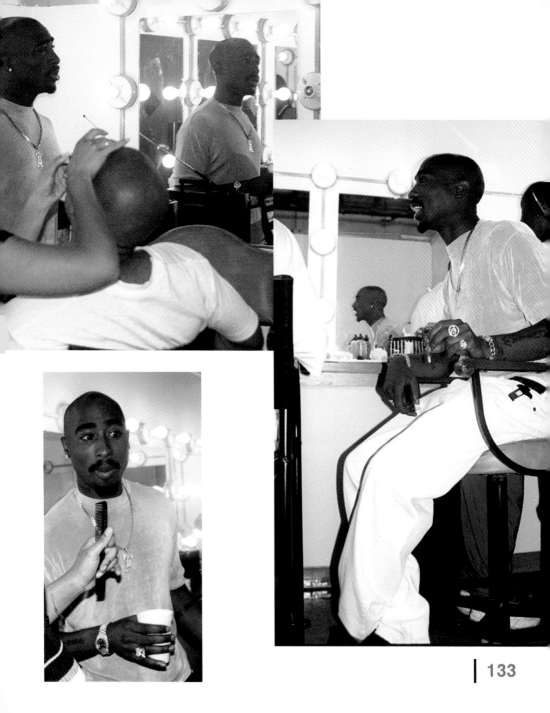

133

Tupac not only trained the Outlawz in regard to music and film, but he was their life coach. His love for them was genuine and apparent.

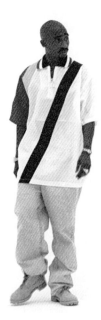

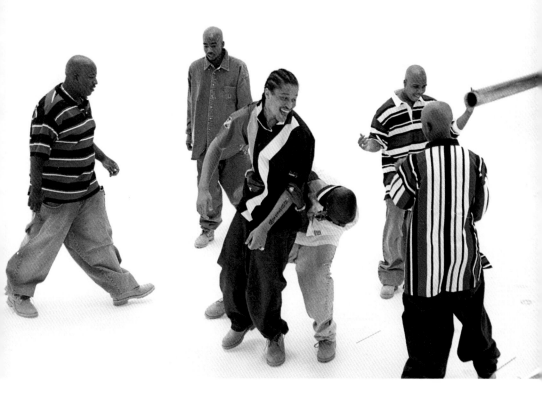

Here Tupac is clowning around with them.

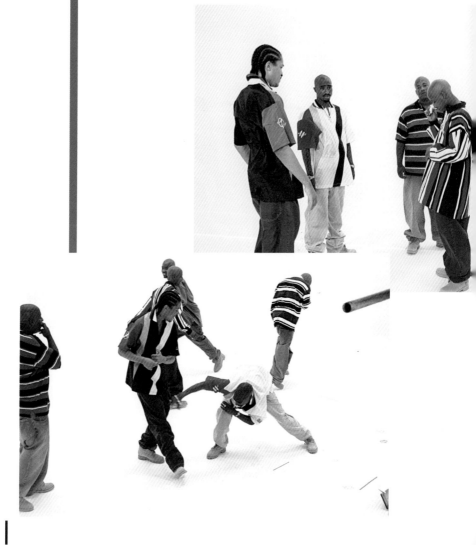

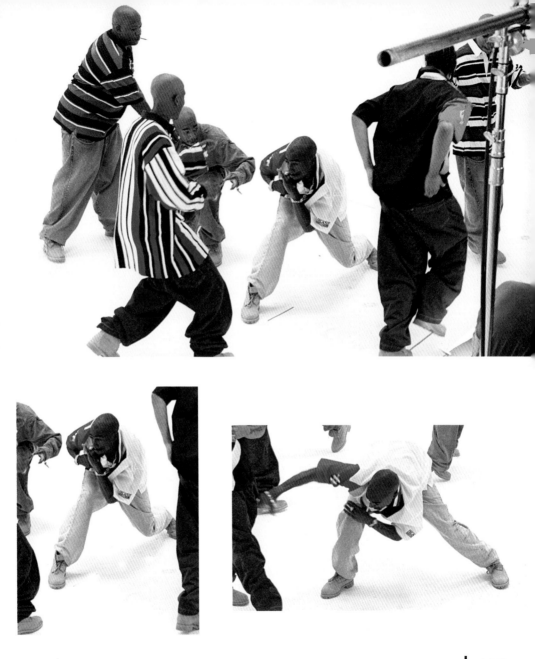

I caught Tupac cooling himself off on the set of the "Hit 'Em Up" video.

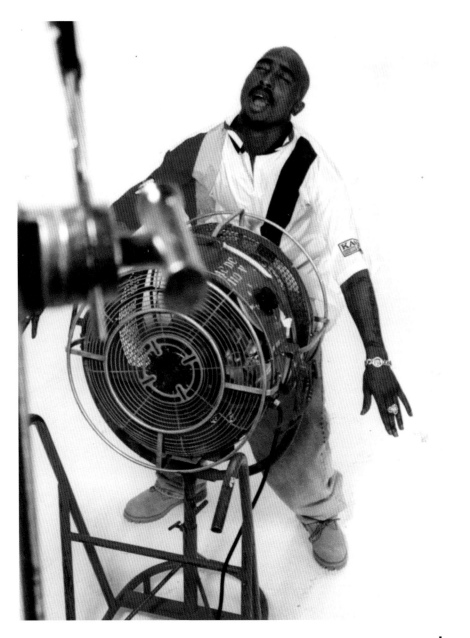

A couple of weeks before the Las Vegas shooting, Suge Knight had invited Tupac there to no avail. On September 7, Tupac agreed to go to the Tyson fight, leaving for Vegas at midday. That date happens to be Tracy's birthday, so I suggested we gather our production crew, rent a passenger van, and head over to celebrate Tracy's birthday with Pac. Tracy loved to be with Tupac but wasn't really into the idea of being around Death Row energy. She eventually succumbed to my stubbornness.

We were planning to meet Tupac at Suge Knight's Club 662 after the Tyson fight. The fact that the spot was filled with thugs and hustlers didn't excite Tracy in the least. We had been milling around for a while, waiting for Tupac to arrive, when Nate Dogg approached us and said that Tupac and Suge had been shot.

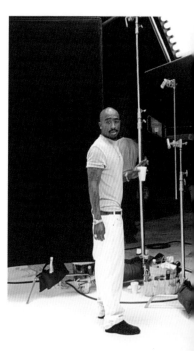

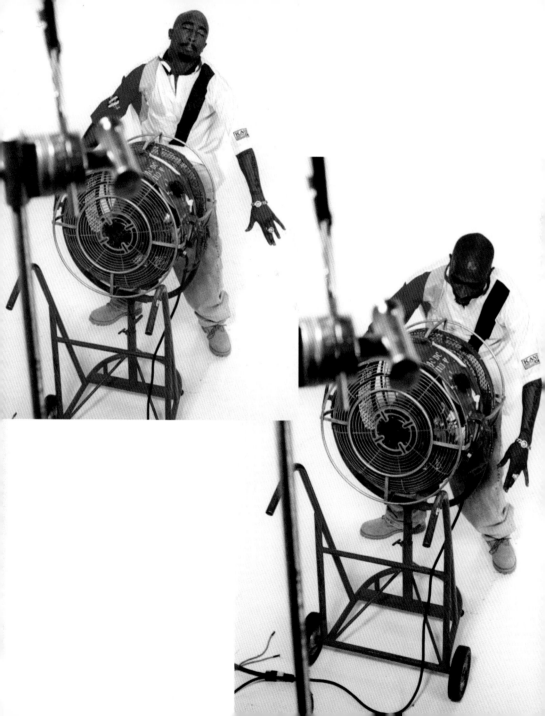

day one
a struggle to survive

Tracy and I made our way to University Medical Center. When we arrived, we saw Tupac's fiancée, Kidada, and his cousin Jamala. Both were talking on the phone and crying. I thought that he must have passed. I soon learned that he was undergoing corrective surgery, but was still in critical condition. That night was one of the longest nights of my life. We stayed through the night and into the next morning.

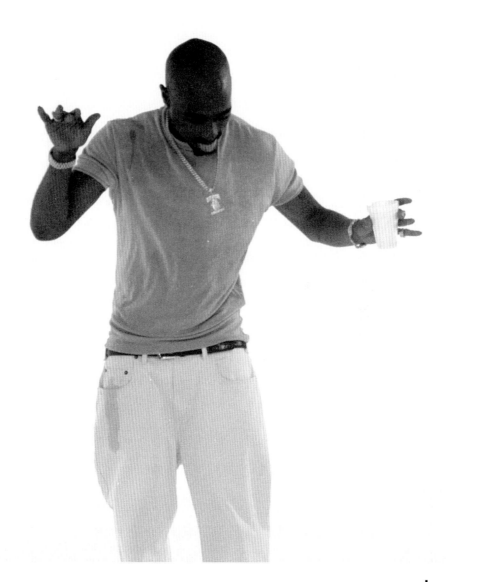

day two
a struggle to survive

I found myself in a daze, staring through the double doors of the emergency room and waiting for something, anything, that would give me hope. I really wanted to go in and see him. Ironically, I felt as though I was back outside the Clinton Correctional Facility. All I could do was pray to God for him. A nurse walked out and told us that he had gone through a very critical evening and although his condition was grave, he was stabilizing. By plane or by car, his loved ones made their way to Las Vegas to be near Tupac's side. Yaasmyn, Molly, the Outlawz, and I set up a twenty-four-hour watch. The hospital administrator gave a news conference, updating the media on Tupac's condition. We prayed as the evening came and went.

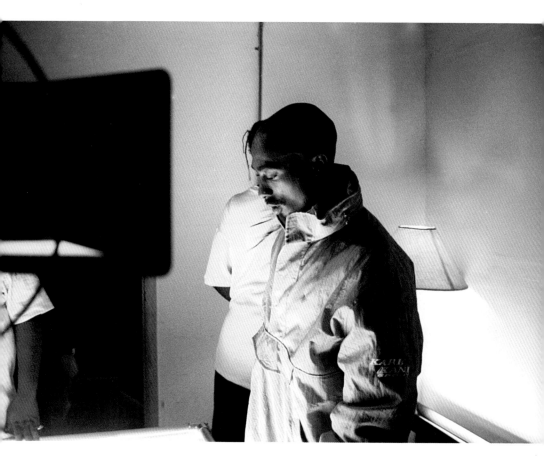

day three
a struggle to survive

In the morning, a nurse told us that they had to sedate Tupac and induce a comalike state because he kept struggling to get out of the bed. The Outlawz, Yaasmyn, Molly, Tracy, and I were like an army at the side of our wounded leader. Tupac's mother and her sister Glo arrived. I had met Afeni once or twice, but we had not yet established a relationship. Her revolutionary past was all I knew about her. She walked into the hospital accompanied by family members. I felt terrible for her. All I could do was think about what my mother would have been going through if I had been lying in that hospital bed. Kidada's mother, Peggy Lipton, arrived at the hospital. It was a sad sight to see Kidada and her mom sitting in their car in the hospital's parking lot.

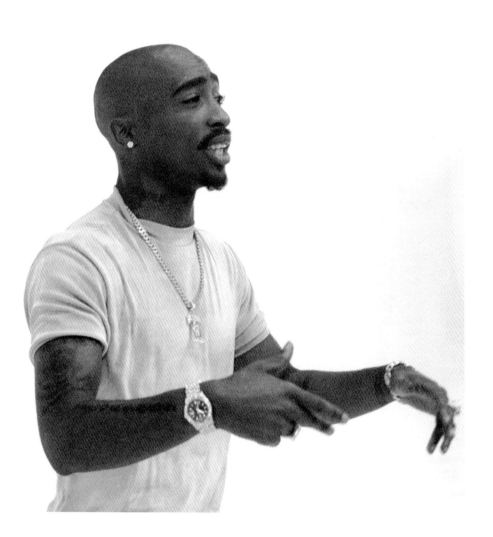

A number of Tupac's friends came to visit him: Yo-Yo, Snoop Dogg, M.C. Hammer, Jasmin Guy, Jesse Jackson, Danny Boy, Mopreme, and many others. Tracy had to go back to L.A. to prep for a music video. Tupac's biological father arrived at the hospital; he didn't have enough money for a hotel room, so I offered to share mine with him. Tupac's condition was still grave and questionable; despite this, we remained hopeful. One of his nurses came to the waiting area around four A.M. and said that she had almost lost him but was able to bring him back after giving him a shot of adrenaline. Standing guard at the hospital was a frightening experience for all of us. There were death threats and myriad unsavory characters milling about. We were able to get the Fruit of Islam to come and stand security. For the first time, it felt a little safer at the hospital.

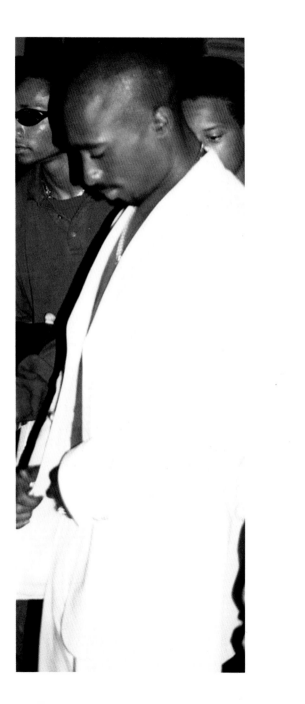

day five
a struggle to survive

The waiting room started to fill up with Tupac's fans. A female reporter posed as a distraught family member and did her best to get information out of me before being escorted out by Molly. At around three A.M. the nurse from the previous night walked up to me and asked if I would like to go in and see him. It would be my first time to see him since the hospital vigil began. I was afraid of what I might see, but nothing could have prepared me for what I did see. Before the shooting, I had only seen Tupac coherent and full of life. When I walked into the hospital room, I saw his bandaged body covered by a thin white sheet, with tubes and machines protruding from all over. Bandages covered his bullet wounds, and one of his fingers was missing. His head was swollen as a result of all the medication they had pumped into him. I walked over and put my hand on his arm. It was cold. I said a prayer and walked silently out of the room.

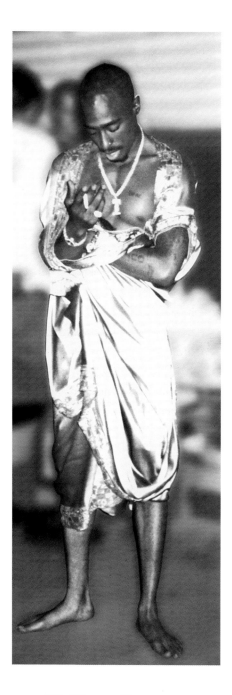

day six
a struggle to survive

The sixth day began the same as the previous five. The nurse came out and told us that Tupac's condition had improved by 13 percent. I called Tracy and gave her the news. She asked me to fly back to L.A. because she needed help on the video she was working on. I decided to say my good-byes to the family and leave. That night was a difficult one for Tracy and me; neither of us could sleep. I felt a tremendous amount of guilt for not being at Tupac's side. All I could do was pray for him.

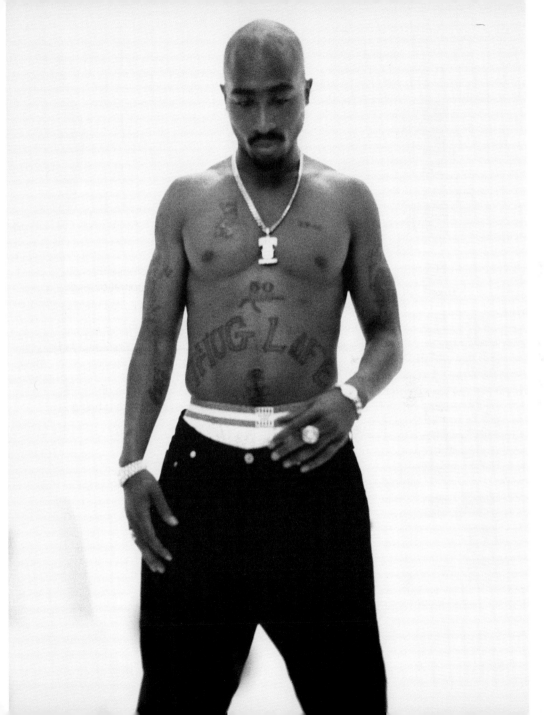

day seven
a struggle to survive

Tracy and I were picked up by our production staff in a van. We were on Interstate 10, on our way to downtown Los Angeles to do a music-video shoot. The only sound in the car was the radio. Theo, a DJ on 92.3 FM "The Beat," announced that Tupac had passed away only a few minutes earlier. The van was silent except for Tracy's feeble cry. I prayed for Tupac's soul and was glad that he was out of pain. September 13, 1996, was one of the saddest days of my life.

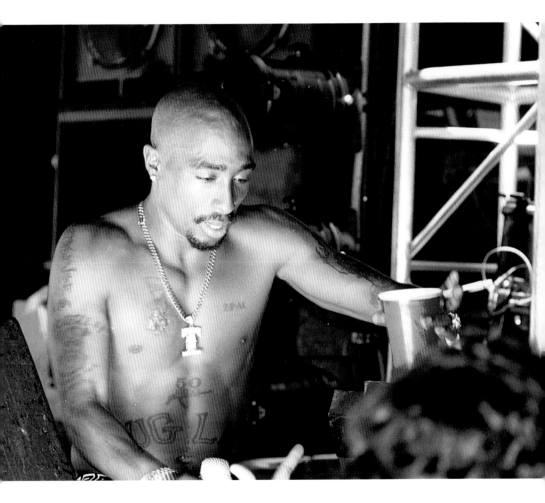

Our final meeting was at Tupac's house in Calabasas, California. Tupac was talking about his future. He said, "In six months, people aren't going to recognize me—I'm going to act like such an adult. In fact, one day I may run for mayor of Los Angeles." Tupac communicates with me to this day. I often think, Jesus died at the age of thirty-three and only a few people knew of him. Tupac died at the age of twenty-five and was known by millions. I wonder how he will be thought of in five hundred or a thousand years. I wish he were still alive.

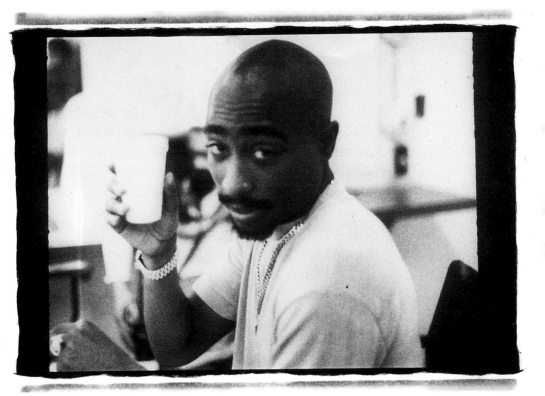

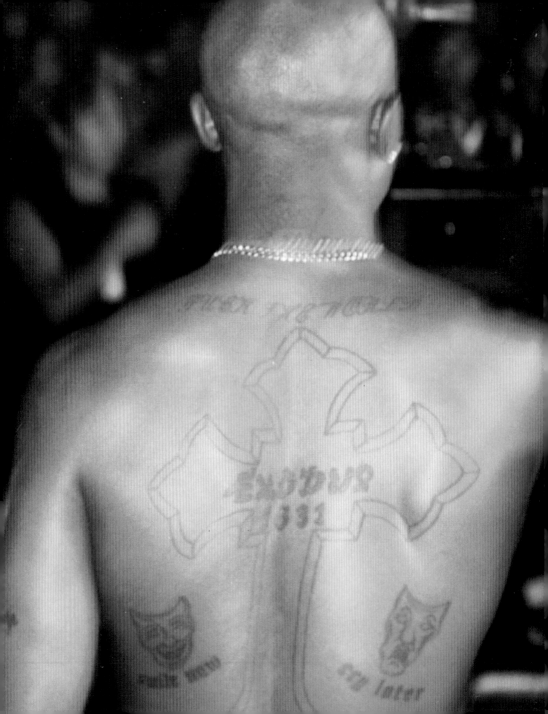